LEARY ON DRUGS

LEARY ON DRUGS

Writings and lectures from Timothy Leary (1970–1996)
Edited by Hassan I. Sirius, with an introduction by R.U. Sirius

RE/Search Editors/Publishers: V. Vale and Marian Wallace
Layout and design: Marian Wallace
Assistant Editor: Emily Epstein
Cover Photograph: Chris Felver
Cover Design: Robert Collison, Jason Ogulnik and Elie Sanh-Ducos
Photographs from Timothy Leary Archive, retouched by RE/Search staff
RE/Search staff: Seth Robson, Emily Epstein, Robert Collison, David Latimer,
    Sandra Derian (proofreader), Scott Bodarky, Jason Ogulnik, Jared Power
Illustrations: Jared Power
Special Thanks: Denis Berry, Michael Horowitz, Dean Metzger
David Latimer, Videobrain

RE/Search Publications
20 Romolo #B
San Francisco, CA 94133
(415) 362-1465

info@researchpubs.com
www.researchpubs.com

Printed in U.S.A. by McNaughton-Gunn
ISBN 978-1-889307-17-6

10   9   8   7   6   5   4   3   2   1

TABLE OF CONTENTS

INTRODUCTION

A friend of mine was having a conversation recently with a 19-year-old woman who was forming some kind of spiritual-psychedelic sex cabal. He mentioned Timothy Leary… and the girl didn't know who he was.

It's probably safe to assume that virtually everyone who purchases this book knows a few things about Timothy Leary. But maybe you were born after the death of history and just happened upon this book. Maybe you saw the photograph of a really happy-looking old dude who's "on drugs" and decided to throw down a few bucks to check it out.

You've stumbled upon an explosive cache of vision and philosophy. This book is—without a doubt—an offer you can't understand… unless you're willing to use your second favorite body part—your brain.

In all seriousness, Dr. Leary would have been thrilled to see these musings on mind-activating substances—some of them carefully crafted essays and a few of them lucid-lunatic ravings—appear under the RE/Search banner, the publisher of brilliant books in collaboration with their hero, William S. Burroughs.

When Leary died on May 31, 1996, TV news programs and newspapers across the land reported on the death of the "acid guru." Leary always hated that term. The truth is, Leary was, arguably, an "acid guru" in the 1960s. In the 1970s, he was a prisoner, an exile, and an early transhumanist (google it). In the '80s and '90s, he was a digital culture enthusiast and vehement anti-authoritarian.

In a late 1980s interview in Canada's newsweekly *MacLeans,* Leary said, "I am 100 % in favor of the intelligent use of drugs, and 1,000 % percent against the thoughtless use of them, whether caffeine or LSD. And drugs are not central to my life."

So, while most of his writings and talks were on other topics, Leary did continue to write and speak articulately, humorously, and on occasion, deliriously—about mind-altering drugs and plants, particularly the psychedelic variety.

For this collection, Hassan I Sirius has edited together Leary's most poetic, insightful, fun, cautious, excessive, reasoned and humorous memoirs, essays and comments about drugs. The book is presented in four sections: Trips, Visions, Theories & Reflections, and Politics of Ecstasy & Infamy, in the hopes that the descriptions of drug experiences and discussions of drug theory and politics will illuminate each other. There are both complete essays and fragments, so if an entry seems to start in the middle of a story or discussion, it's not the Nitrous Oxide speaking. Hassan put it together that way.

A few psychedelic seekers may come to this tome in hopes of finding the words of an enlightened master who can show them the way to perfect illumination and lead them into the "New Age." If that's you, you've come to the right place… to be disabused of that sort of b.s. This book shows that Leary was brilliant, but like all of us, flawed—and more importantly, it challenges you to take responsibility for your own brain, and not to hand it over to the state, the gurus, Dr. Phil, Tom Cruise, or Timothy Leary.

Leary's main fault, and it's mostly a lovable one, is probably an excess of optimism. Indeed, the assumption that forms the core of Leary's writings about drugs—particularly psychedelic drugs—is that nearly all who try them will find the experience extraordinary and at least a bit meaningful. During the 1960s, the culture around acid and its psychedelic cousins encouraged this search for meaning; this sensitivity to the experience; this openness to being awed. *Oh wow!*

But after that psychedelic explosion, as psychedelic drugs and psyche-delia drifted more quietly through American culture, psychedelic experience has become—in some ways—just one more data point in an oncoming, overwhelming, and mostly pointless memetic flood. A fair number of people who have grown up in this accelerated, chaotic, painfully grotesque and bizarre culture seem to take acid and say: "Yeah... *and?*" But this may actually be because most people today are taking small doses. Those walloping, mind-melting, awe-inspiring 500 microgram doses of yesteryear are, for the most part, a thing of the past (and perhaps, the future).

Let's put Dr. Leary's psychedelic enthusiasms into context. Each generation since the sixties has also produced a couple of hundred thousand sensitive, smart mutants who take drugs seriously. And with a plethora of promising scientific and psychological studies once again proving the therapeutic and visionary value of hallucinogens, we may soon see various psychedelics advertised on TV as psychiatric drugs that promise to cure post-industrial malaise. ("Possible side effects include nausea, vomiting, ego death, tree hugging, and a sudden disbelief in nation states and boundaries. Consult immediately with your doctor and the nearest Department of Homeland Security official if these symptoms should occur.")

In 1984, Leary wrote, "Acid should not be taken by scared persons or in a fearful setting. America is a spooked country these days. The genetic caste of danger-criers is operating in full voice. Never in our history has the national mood been so gloomy and spooky." Dude, you had no clue just how gloomy and spooky it was going to get.

Still, maybe this is just the right time for American to embark on a new wave of Xtreme psychedelic freaking. After the '50s, America needed a big psychic enema, and Dr. Leary came to the rescue. Seems like we might be due for another visit to the Doctor. Just don't ask me to hold the bag. Do It Yourself!

This book is a good place to start.

R.U. SIRIUS
APRIL 1, 2008

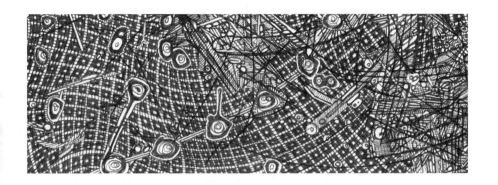

Chapter One
TRIPS

First Trip: Look Ma, No Drug

Spain, 1959

In 1959, I sailed for Spain on the S.S. Independence, American Export Lines, with my two children, Susan, age nine, and Jack, age seven.

We settled in a villa in Torremolinos on the Costa del Sol. There the kids trooped off across the field to school each morning while I stayed home to die messily.

The coast of Spain—Malaga to Gibraltar—is the southernmost part of Europe, and down to this bottom sift and fall the psychological dregs of the Continent—drunken Swedes, cashiered Danes, twisted Germans, sodden Brits.

The main occupation of the Torremolinos colony was drug taking and the drug was alcohol.

I had brought with me a trunk full of psychological data, thousands of test scores and numerical indices that demonstrated with precision why psychotherapy did not work. In America, I had a staff of statisticians and clerks and rooms of calculators and computers to handle the data. But I had said good-bye to all that and sat sweating in a small room in a Spanish house adding and subtracting long columns of figures—hour after hour.

It was a brutal yoga. Each laborious calculation was proving that psychology was just a mind-game, an eccentric head trip on the part of psychologists, and that psychotherapy was an arduous, expensive, ineffective, unimaginative attempt to impose the mind of the doctor on the mind of the patient.

Each arithmetical index was pushing me farther and farther from my chosen profession.

The dying process was slow.

I would throw down the ballpoint pen and walk fast to the main street of the village and sit in a bar and drink and talk in detached-zombie-fashion with the expatriates and leave abruptly and run back to the house to continue the paralyzing calculations, sweating in panic.

Boredom, black depression, flashes of frantic, restless anxiety. No place to go.

In December the rains came and the Mediterranean was gray and cold. On Christmas Eve I met a young, runaway prostitute from Valencia and took her home. By New Years I had the clap.

In the middle of January, I moved with the kids to a steam-heated hotel, but Jack's un-house-trained puppy and my distant gloom freaked the owner, so I moved to an apartment tunneled into the rock at the foot of Calle San Miguel. It was a cave with oozing stone walls. The beds were always damp.

There the breakthrough/breakdown started.

It began in the head. One morning my scalp began to itch. By noon it was unbearable. Each hair root was a burning rod of sensation. My hair was a cap of fire. I ran down the beach and cut my feet on rocks to keep from ripping my fingers through my scalp.

By evening my face began to swell and huge water blisters erupted from my cheeks. A young Danish doctor came, injected me with a huge needle, and gave me sleeping pills.

In the morning I was blind—eyes shut tight by swollen tissue and caked with dried pus. I felt my way to the bathroom, lit a candle, and pried open one eye before the mirror.

In the oblong glass I saw the twisted, tormented face of an insane stranger.

A Spanish doctor came and gave me more shots and more sleeping pills. He had never seen such a case before. Jack and Susan crept into the room to look at me with big sorrowful eyes. The bed was cold and soggy but I slept.

The third day the disease had spread to my body. Huge watery welts blossomed on my back, stomach, and flanks. Both the Danish and the Spanish doctors shook their heads, and both gave me injections from large metal hypodermics.

In the afternoon I hired a taxi and was driven to Malaga to consult a specialist. His eyes bulged and he shook his head and gave me two injections.

Before returning to Torremolinos, I sat at a sidewalk cafe and drank a Coca-Cola. A pretty young Swedish girl joined me. She was traveling with her parents and was bored and rebellious, hungry for adventure. She steamed with erotic vapor. I looked at her and smiled weakly. See you later.

Back at Torremolinos, the doctors agreed I should move to a steam-heated hotel. We had to smuggle the dog in. Jack and Susan left to stay with a sabbatical family from the University of Pennsylvania.

By night the disease had spread to my extremities. My wrists and hands were swollen to arthritic paralysis. My ankles and feet ballooned. I couldn't walk or move my fingers. I sat in the darkness for several hours and then came the scent of decay. Overpowering odor of disintegration.

I got up from the chair, but my feet buckled and I fell to my knees. I crawled across the room to the electric switch and pulled myself up to flick on the light.

> I died. I let go. Surrendered.
> I slowly let every tie to my old life slip
> away. My career, my ambitions, my home.
> My identity. The guilts. The wants.

Jack's puppy had been very sick and a rivulet of yellow shit ran along the floor. I would be expelled from the hotel if the chambermaid found the evidence. I crawled to the bathroom and pulled down a roll of toilet paper. For the next hour I crept along the tile floor cleaning up the mess. It was slimy mucus, the color of peanut butter.

I crawled to the bathroom. The toilet didn't work. I crawled to the window, which overlooked the back yard of the hotel and heaved out the wad of toilet paper.

There were electric wires about four feet below the window and the discolored strings of paper caught on the wires and hung down like banners swaying in the breeze. Flag of my action.

Using an umbrella as a cane, I hobbled along the hallway, down the back stairs, and across the rutted muddy back yard. Each step was torture. I fell several times. I stood on a packing crate and flailed at the paper banner like a madman fighting vultures.

By the time I wrenched back to the room, two hours had elapsed. I was weak and trembling. I slumped in the chair for the rest of the dark night, wrapped in a Burberry mackintosh.

I died. I let go. Surrendered.

I slowly let every tie to my old life slip away. My career, my ambitions, my home. My identity. The guilts. The wants.

With a sudden snap, all the ropes of my social self were gone. I was a thirty-eight-year-old male animal with two cubs. High, completely free.

I could feel some seed of life stirring inside, and energy uncoiling. When the dawn came, I moved my hands. The swelling was gone. I found a pen and paper. I wrote three letters. One to my employers, telling them I was not returning to my job. A second went to my insurance agent to cash in my policies. And a third long manuscript went to a colleague, spelling out certain revelations about the new psychology, the limiting artifactual nature of the mind, the unfolding possibilities of mind-free consciousness, the liberating effect of the ancient rebirth process that comes only through death of the mind.

The ordeal in Spain was the first of some 400 death-rebirth trips I have experienced since 1958. This first trip was non-chemical. Or was it?

First High Dose Psilocybin Trip
Massachusetts, 1960

> Scenario: Leary's first psychedelic drug trip on psilocybin in Mexico has been retold in most of his books and elsewhere in biographies and in histories of the 1960s. This is a different story—about his first high dose psilocybin trip, months later at his home in Newton Center, Massachusetts while still a professor at Harvard. His 12-year-old daughter Susan is having a pajama party, and after the girls head up to Susan's bedroom, Leary's friend Charlie convinces him and another man, O'Donell to take some psilocybin. Leary had just received his first supply from Sandoz Laboratories in Switzerland for use in his Harvard Psilocybin Research Project, and he was trying very hard not to indulge in extracurricular dosing. However, mildly tipsy from cocktails, the gentlemen wind up wolfing down quite a few more pills than usual. —Editor

From all the literature I had read on the subject, my friends and I had just surpassed the world's record for psilocybin consumption. The psychiatric people had been using 8 to 10 milligrams (that is, four to five pills), and I had just consumed 20 milligrams (ten pills) and so had O'Donell, and Charlie had wolfed down 22 milligrams.

It hit in about twenty minutes, the waves of sensation rippling down the body and the pressure on the eardrums. There were six doors to the kitchen and they were all closed. We were sealed in a bathysphere plunged down to sea bottom. The walls and ceilings glowed phosphorescent yellow—an electric, vibrating color. The floor was shimmering like lemon Jell-O. Some torn fragments of party decorations were scattered on the floor and they sparkled—dazzling, black, shiny ebony jewels. Orange gems.

Some kid had left a cardboard top hat and Charlie tilted it on his head. His face was huge, yellow-stained with deep green shadows under his eyes. He had grown in stature, the leader, the keeper of the mushrooms. Top-hatted ringmaster of the cosmic circus. Chuckling, grinning impishly. Walking around the kitchen joking about the fortune in jewels on the floor, lifting his huge body in a comic tiptoe gait. The clown genius. He was the wisest and funniest person I had ever seen.

> ## Then suddenly it all changes. The play has started. We are puppets in an old cosmological drama.

O'Donell, the rebel, was in a good mood too. We were three kitchen conspirators. Three gods romping around a spangly paradise. There were only the three of us in the yellow-walled universe. No one else existed but this rolling trinity. Then over the laughter I heard a noise, a door opening upstairs and a blast of rock-and-roll from the record player, and then the door closing and silence. Oh yes; from a thousand years back I remembered the party and the girls' slumber-group upstairs on that other distant planet. Vague angst. Are they all right? Are they doing well a million light-years away up there? Yes. Don't worry. Don't take the interstellar trip up there to see . . .

Then suddenly it all changes. The play has started. We are puppets in an old cosmological drama.

Scene One: A large entrance hall leading to wide sweeping stairs. On the left of the stairs a huge oaken door closes off the dining room. On the right an archway leads into an enormous living room, dimly lit. A small door leading into the kitchen is shut. The floor and stairs are covered with a deep-piled rug, no, it is really a desert expanse of sand. A wide stream of brown sand silently runs down the stairs and flows into a shifting pool on the hallway floor. The top half of the front door is set in polished diamond, three feet by five feet, flashing intense glass light. The woodwork and closet doors are carved ivory, solid, bone smooth and cool to the touch. A light green silk covers the walls and in the fabric are thousands of yellow diamonds in the form of *fleur de lis* gleaming. A golden picture frame outlines a large rectangular hole in the wall. Within the hole, about three feet back, sits a tall Spanish cardinal. He has a long, thin, dirty white beard, which trembles as he breathes. An elongated El Greco nose and deep-set eyes watch steadily, now frowning, now smiling, now turning down to the illuminated manuscript on which his hands rest and along which his slender fingers move. His thin body is covered with the red folds of an Episcopal robe, with his arms in yellow-white lace. He is watching, waiting, judging, preparing to render verdict.

On the opposite wall, there hangs a four-foot Moroccan mosque lamp, burnished gold, pierced over its entire swollen surface with filigreed lacework designs. Inside the lamp, behind orange, red, and green glass, burn three bulbs spilling colors over the wall, setting fire to the green silk and reflecting from the embedded, flowered diamonds.

The sand below the lamp is littered with piles of gems—ruby, emerald, orange-diamond, which have dropped down through the latticed holes.

Spotlights flood the stage with changing waves of color. Under the sand floor is an electric generator, which emits a steady hum and charges the atmosphere with high-voltage currents.

For centuries there is no action, only the cardinal moving his thin fingers across his scrolled pages and breathing softly.

Then . . .

The kitchen door opens. Enter Charlie, pagan leader of the rebel gang. He is nine feet tall, a mountain man with a huge meat-red face glowing with energy, grinning, chuckling over some rebel-triumph, eyes dancing. His black top hat is tilted. He doesn't walk. He soars in leaping, floating, and steps to center stage, looking around in pleased admiration. He turns and beckons to his two followers.

Enter O'Donell and Leary. They are small, wiry, happy rebels. O'Donell's face is covered with freckled potato sacking through which his white animal teeth gleam with impish pleasure. Leary gazes around in wonder.

Leader Charlie floats halfway up the stairs and sweeps his hand round in gesture.

charlie: Look. Look at the emeralds. Look at the gold. Look at the diamonds.

Leary stands in dazed awe. O'Donell shuffles around the stage, his shoulders butting forward. He is grinning fiercely.

o'donell: They left them and now it's all ours. [All three roar with laughter.] Quick, get a paper bag and we'll scoop up all those jewels.

charlie: And the sand. Look, rivers of it. The owners of this house are going to be surprised to find this desert in their hall-way. [All laugh. And laugh.] What can we do with it?

leary: Tell the people who take care of the house to sweep it up. And clean up all these sloppy piles of jewels scattered around. Bad housekeeping. [All laugh. And laugh.] Tell them to put the sand into millions of hourglasses.

charlie: Hourglasses. What are they for?

leary: I once heard about people who make machines to meas-ure time.

charlie: Measure time! They think they can measure time?

o'donell: Hah. Measure time? What crazy thing will they think of next?

leary: Why sure. People will sell the jewels to buy machines to measure time.

charlie: Sell jewels? Next you know they'll be selling sunshine.

leary: And moonlight.

o'donell: I am time. Can they measure me? With an hourglass?

All laugh. And laugh.

Charlie soars down from the stairs and bounds around the stage. O'Donell and Leary follow him aimlessly.

charlie: This stage is so empty.

leary: Yes, big and empty.

o'donell: They've all gone.

charlie: Where did they go?

o'donell: They've been doing it forever.

leary: Yes, they do, don't they.

charlie: What? Do what?

o'donell: Come and act on the stage set for a while and then go.

charlie: Why do they do it?

o'donell: Nobody has ever figured it out.

Leary has been standing studying the jewels dropping from the burnished mosque lamp. He turns with a start.

leary: Figured what out?

o'donell: Where they come from. Why they come. Where they're going.

They stand, all three, in silence for . . . well, let's say eleven years. Then the cardinal sitting behind the gold frame in his rectangle cave turns and raises his left hand up to his chin so that it covers, merges with his elongated beard. His eyes smile compassionately. He speaks in a low voice in Spanish.

cardinal: Dear little ones. Do you really think that you can answer that riddle?

leary: Can you answer it?

The cardinal smiles, moves his arm down to the book, exposing his beard, then moves it back, tugging softly at his chin. He says nothing.

leary: Yes, I can answer the riddle. There is no riddle. He is thinking of each grain in the river of sand swirling below his feet.

o'donell: That's right, there's no riddle. I've solved it all, many times.

charlie: [Reproachful leader-god, commanding.] Why do you guys worry? With all this beauty? Why worry about riddles?

o'donell: What riddles?

charlie: Exactly. What riddles?

o'donell: We were talking about all of them and where they went.

charlie: Who?

o'donell: Why, all the actors that were here before.

charlie: It is funny when you think about it. Where did they go? Who?

leary: Well, there were the Landlords. They rented us the house and left. They think they own the set.

o'donell: Own the set? Own?

leary: And the land too. They think they own the land. [All laugh. And laugh.]

charlie: [Still laughing.] Stop it you guys. It's too much. You make it sound like a game of Monopoly. Own the land. [He laughs.]

leary: Damn right. They bought it with money, too.

o'donell: Money, hah.

charlie: Money. You mean the green paper that you find in the cardboard box that the game comes in.

leary: Exactly.

charlie: Good. Now I understand.

leary: Well, the Landlords bought it from the Cartwrights. And the Crabtrees, they sold it to the Cartwrights. That was much earlier in the game.

o'donell : All gone.

leary: And here we are. With all the sand and the jewels and the ivory that goes with it.

o'donell: Well I think it's only right that we keep up the game. Why don't we buy it and sell it to each other?

charlie: Yeah, good idea. It will pass the time. And then after we get tired buying and selling let's go in and listen to music in the study. [Short pause. Charlie now leaps back up on the stairs.] It really is beautiful, isn't it? Shimmering and glowing.

o'donell: Strange, strange.

leary: Yes. What?

o'donell: That they did it all. The stage is set.

charlie: [Soaring down to the doors.] You mean the way they made these ivory doors?

o'donell: Yes. Look at them. How they worked!

leary: And how they cared. They must have cared.

charlie: And the old Arab lamp there. Some old Arab sitting in his tent hammering it and designing the holes and lacework.

leary: And all for us.

o'donell: They made the scene and left.

charlie: Left it for us.

o'donell: [Pointing.] Hey, why is that big door to the dining room shut? I hate shut doors.

charlie: It's stuck. I tried to open it.

o'donell: How did it get closed in the first place?

leary: I shut it during the game.

o'donell: What game?

leary: The game where the boys were searching blind after the girls. I had the boys shut up in there while the girls were hiding and it got stuck.

o'donell: [He bends over shaking his head, wolf-like and muttering.] Always a mistake.

leary: What?

o'donell: To shut people in. Always a mistake.

charlie: [The leader.] Well, let's open the bars. Freedom. The three of us can push the gate back.

Charlie motions. O'Donell and Leary float over and they begin shoving and butting, trying to slide the door along its roller. It doesn't move. They try again. Then stop, all leaning in pushing positions against the door.

leary: Well, we've been able to open lots of things up tonight. But this one we can't do.

charlie: Yeah. Can't win them all. We'll do it tomorrow when we're not under . . . when we feel stronger.

o'donell: [He is frowning and gnashing his teeth slowly, hunched over.] Well, I feel strong now. Stronger than anyone in the world. And I want doors open. I can't stand to be cooped in.

He starts pushing violently, savagely, his eyes gleaming and his teeth white against his brown, cloth face. He can't move the door. Failure makes him angrier and he throws himself against the door again growling.

The colored floodlights begin to dim and the room grows shadowy. Jewels lose their sparkle. The gem shadows are puddles of drab color. Sand river turns into tan stained carpet. The white ivory woodwork gleams unpleasantly bright. Charlie becomes an ungainly young man, silly with child's hat on his head. Three drugged men in disheveled shirtsleeves wandering around at the foot of the wide, sweeping staircase.

The bearded cardinal has frozen, two-dimensional against the wall. Three Beckett clowns on a vast, empty stage. Pointlessly milling around.

I heard O'Donell saying something about the teenage girls upstairs. I frowned. Bad thought. Keep the other planets out of the action. Charlie tilted his top hat down over his eyes, giggling at O'Donell. No point in thinking about girls, O'Donell, you're impotent under the drug anyway. O'Donell scowled. Oh yeah. That's what you think. Talk about your own impotency but it doesn't hold for me. I may turn them on.

Leary has been standing studying the jewels dropping from the burnished mosque lamp.

Charlie grinned. What would the girls' mothers think if they knew there were drugged men roving around the house? The girls have never been safer, I said. All the reports say that the drug turns sex off. Charlie laughed. That's right. Last night I could look at Rhona and Joan and they were beautiful but I had no lust and didn't even want to touch them.

O'Donell loosed a mocking laugh. The scene bothered me. I was feeling disjointed and rudderless. I felt a longing for someone loving. I missed Joan and wanted to hold her close. Charlie and O'Donell were arguing and the happy mood was lost. Life is pointless without love, I said. We're straggling, lost on an endless desert stage. It's all meaningless, but we have to do something.

O'Donell leered. Speak for yourself. I'm going upstairs.

It was crystal clear to me that life without love is an empty sham, senseless action, puppetry. But we have to do something. What had any point? I tried to use my mind, but there were no categories, no clichés, nothing inferential to hold on to. All loveless actions were ritual. Empty gestures. Where... where is the real right program? What, what to do and why? Where to begin? How to build up a life of loveless action? I was standing in the hallway with my eyes closed trying to find a philosophy, a way, a meaning. What is life about anyway, without love? I was pushing my mind back, back to some beginnings, to something basic. What action is any better than the other? What? What? What? Painful, clutching conflict. Then I reached something. Helping others. Yes, that's the beginning.

Everywhere there is hurtfulness and then we try to help. Yes. There's a difference that makes sense. It is better to help than hurt. The house is a mess from the party. Rhona will have to clean it up tomorrow. I'll do it tonight. That makes sense. I'll start with the kitchen.

Charlie and O'Donell were still bantering sarcastically at the foot of the stairs. The only loveless action that makes sense is to clean up the mess, I said. Matter of fact, that's a form of love. Come on out and help me.

I left them and walked into the kitchen and started running water in the sink and rinsing dishes. The door opened and Charlie walked in. O'Donell's gone upstairs. Upstairs? I thought of upstairs and I thought of the girls and the slumber party. Waves of guilt washed over me for having dragged my kids around from country to country, school to school, house to house, and Susan missing friends and the warm, cozy routine schedule and this was her first party, her first social event, and how excited she was and nothing must mar it, no clowning-around adults. Upstairs? Where did he go upstairs? To bed. I turned from the sink and looked at Charlie. My voice was harsh. Are you sure?

Charlie's face reacted to my rough tones. A look of terror. Yes, well, I'm sure . . . that's what he said. My voice ominous. Well, I gave you the pills and it's your party and you're responsible. More terror. Gee, I'll go upstairs to check. I stood by the sink thinking again about the dear, naive, tender daughter, wanting so much a normal stable growing up. I dried my hands and started upstairs. In the upper hallway I could see the door to the girls' room open and Charlie's voice commanding. I was sick with the horror of it. O'Donell, drugged, lurching into the slumber party. Scandal. Susan's dream of social acceptance shattered. The girls were standing in the center of the room bug-eyed. O'Donell was lying on their bed. Charlie was bending over him pulling his arm. Come on O'Donell, let's go downstairs. O'Donell's mocking sneer. Nah. I doan wanna go downstairs. I'm gonna stay here with the girls.

Charlie had pulled him up to a sitting position. Come on, O'Donell, you can't be in here. Nah. Who says I can't. I do what I like. I grabbed his other arm and we yanked him to his feet. O'Donell tried to throw us off but we held on. Come on, O'Donell. We don't belong here. This is the girls' party. Look at Susie. You love her, don't you? Do you want to spoil her party? I looked at Susan. She was watching us silently, curiously. We pulled O'Donell out the door. He was struggling but not too hard. We hustled him to the other end of the hallway and stopped. "Goddammit, O'Donell, knock it off. You have no right to butt in there."

O'Donell's words hit my empty mind like hammer strokes.

Charlie and I were towering over him. He was shrinking back from us, his eyes glaring, his lips drawn back in animal rage. I had never seen such a visage of evil. He gnashed his teeth. He had shrunk in size and was crouching, possessed with malice. Shocking awful evil. Cornered rat, cornered rat was running through my mind.

"Neah. Neah." Mocking whine. "Who are you to say what is right? Maybe I know what's right for those girls. Pampered middle-class dears in there, watching television and playing records, growing up to be miserable middle-class bitches. Maybe the greatest thing that can happen to them in their life is for me to stir them up a little."

O'Donell's words hit my empty mind like hammer strokes. Stunned me. "My God, maybe he's right. What reason, real reason do I have to interfere? It's my own dirty mind." I was racking my brain looking for a moral rebuttal. I was on Mars, you understand, looking down at earth, seeing in a flash the absurdity of social fears, taboos, the insane rituals that enslave mankind, the horrid middle-class fear. The fear. The fear. Did I want to descend to Main Street and protect tribal codes? Identify with the New England middle class? Share their insane terror of nonconformity? Their fear? I felt somehow that what O'Donell was doing was wrong, but I couldn't tell him why. My mind had been purged of cliché and irrational belief. The beautiful, pure empty mind faced with the existential moment. The moral crisis. Why shouldn't O'Donell do what he wanted? Who could tell in the long run whether his plan would or would not be good? He might be the sharp Zen master to shake the girls out of middle-class shackles.

I turned, puzzled, to Charlie. He was standing, holding O'Donell's arm. His face was dazed. "Tell him, Charlie, why he shouldn't go into the girls' room." Charlie stared at me. "I ... I don't know why it's wrong for him to go there."

I could tell that Charlie was going through the same moral search. "Listen, Charlie. Don't you think it's wrong for him to go back in the girls' room?" Charlie nodded decisively. "Yes. I know it's wrong." "Well, Charlie, tell him why it's wrong." Again the puzzled, helpless look. "I ... I ... I can't tell him. I don't know why. I can't think of any reason."

Plunged back into the cosmic vacuum. My mind ran through a hundred conventional, clichéd reasons and rejected them. O'Donell was smiling with mean triumph. "You see, you can't tell me I'm wrong. Do you want to set yourselves up as the great moralists? Telling me about your miserable shoulds and shouldn'ts." O'Donell made a move down the hall. Charlie and I grabbed him.

"Wait a minute. I know you shouldn't go there. I can't tell you why, but I know you're wrong."

I felt the need for someone present who was not under the drugs. We were still the only three men in the universe and we needed help.

It was all perfectly clear to me. We were recapitulating the moral struggles of the human race. We were the first and only men on earth and we were faced with the first ethical decision. Of course we could use force. Charlie and I, the first cosmic police force, could bend his arms and drag him—the first and eternal criminal—away, and overpower him. By force. But why? What justification besides force? It was the first original moral choice of my life. The first time I was faced with a fresh, ethical crossroads. There was no learned, easy motto to parrot. Ethics had to be built right up from scratch and it had to be right not in terms of revealed dogma, or fear of punishment, but in terms of the basic issue. Now what was the basic issue? What is the unassailable first assumption? Suddenly it came to me. Moses on the mountain. A beautiful bolt of Rightness.

"*I'll* tell you why you can't go into Susan's room. Because it is her trip, her territory, her party, and because she doesn't want you there. You have the right to do anything you want to so long as you don't force your trip on anyone else. No one has the right to force himself on someone else against his will." I was speaking slowly with the greatest seriousness. When I finished, Charlie shouted, "Yes, of course, that's exactly right. You can't go there because the girls don't want you. Do your own thing. Let them do their thing.

Tremendous flood of relief. The first ethical law had been forged. Moses smiles. There was a right—not based on force, not based on fear, not based on irrational taboo or custom or dogma. But based on cellular equality. Mutual respect. Charlie and I were nodding at each other happily. O'Donell was making a mocking growling noise and suddenly he burst out of our grasp and started down the hall. We grabbed him and pulled him back and around the corner to the North wing of the house far away from the girls.

O'Donell was seething with futile rage. Again the rat-face and fangs, and his face even seemed gray and furry. We stood there blocking his way, arguing. "You're cops. All cops are the same. Telling me what I can't do." Charlie and I were reasoning with him. "Why don't we go back downstairs and have fun the way we were?" Charlie was pleading. He had been swayed by O'Donell's violent rebuttal. We got no place—we were spoilsport, busybody policemen and O'Donell was going to have his own way. "What can we do?" Charlie was looking at me pleading.

Suddenly I felt a moral impatience with Charlie. He was no longer the wise, Olympian clown god. He was a whining, begging boy who had talked me into giving him the pills and caused all this mess. "Goddammit, Charlie. See what you did giving out the pills that way? I never wanted you to start this mess. You were the big shot and it's your responsibility."

Now Charlie was mad. "Oh? It's my responsibility, is it? Well, I quit! I resign! You're twice my age and you're twice as smart as I am and you handle it. I quit!" Charlie dropped O'Donell's arm and started down the back stairs to the kitchen. "Good," said O'Donell, "all the cops quit and now I'm going back to see the girls." O'Donell started down the north-wing hallway and Charlie was moving down the stairs. I was panicked. I could follow O'Donell and leap on him and wrestle him back, but I feared the noise. I was obsessed by the dread of disturbing the girls. Fear of a scandal. I called down the stairs. Now I was pleading. "Okay, Charlie. It's not your responsibility. But as one friend to another, as one human being to another, will you help me keep him away from the girls?"

Charlie looked up in my eyes. We both understood. Responsibility and roles were nonsensical and Charlie had been right to see through this and reject it. Under the mushrooms there aren't roles and rituals. But the appeal to him as man to man couldn't be dismissed. Charlie bounded back up and ran to the corner of the hall. He grabbed O'Donell's arm. O'Donell snarled and tried to push past. Charlie laughed, ominous, confident. "Oh, little man, you want to get rough with me?" Football Charlie was a giant pushing back the tiny foe. "Don't try to pull any force, O'Donell, because that just won't work."

The three of us standing in the north-wing hallway, O'Donell sunk in bitter passivity. He was still muttering about cops. I felt the need for someone present who was not under the drugs. We were still the only three men in the universe and we needed help. Then I thought of Rhona. "Charlie, go up and wake Rhona. Tell her we need her down here badly." Charlie nodded and started down the hall. He walked sheepishly and I shouted to him (again sore about his giving out the mushrooms irresponsibly), "Ah ha, you're guilty, aren't you?" I was happy to see him guilty at waking his wife and exposing her to this drug mess. I was happy because it made me right and him wrong.

> ## Could she give a reason, a rule that went beyond the transient rules of the games that we all knew we didn't have to play?

Rhona's face was pinched and sour. She was blinking at the light. I was glad to see her. Rhona, a terrible thing has happened. She was cool and business-like: "What's so terrible?" I explained the situation. First of all, you must realize that the three of us have taken a bigger dose of these pills than anyone in the world. Rhona was still cool. So what's so bad about that?

Then I told her about the scene in the girls' room and how O'Donell insisted on going back. Rhona listened calmly and thoughtfully and we were all watching her. She became the great judge and lawgiver.

"Who says I shouldn't do what I want to do?" "But, teenage girls! Susan's party!" We were pleading our cases. Rhona listened. The hallway was shadowy, a dim cave deep in the underworld. We finished. Finally the silence breaks. Truth speaks. "Of course you can't go in there, O'Donell!

And his voice came back, mocking Rhona's prim, proper British, "Nyayah. Why can't I go in there? What law says I can't, and whose law?"

My tight muscles loosened when Rhona had pronounced the verdict, but now they tightened again. Could she give a reason, a rule that went beyond the transient rules of the games that we all knew we didn't have to play?

And the reply, cool and so convincing. Impossible to think of going in there, O'Donell. "Grown-ups don't join pajama parties! It just isn't done."

Wham! What a judgment. What legal logic. Moses, take your stone tablets. Justice Brandeis, forget your Blackstone. Rhona's words. Pinnacle of legal reasoning. Rhona, just two years out of teenage herself, knew the rule as relentless as three strikes you're out. Adults don't infringe on the trip of the adolescent. I was swinging clear and happy. And loving Rhona. Admiration. O'Donell was stunned. You could see his tense squirming body begin to relax. Looking down at the floor. Nodding his head. We stood for a long time and then Rhona, briskly, case-dismissed, no-nonsense voice said, "All right. All of you come down to the kitchen and I'll brew up some tea and cookies."

Rhona went up to check in on the pajama party while the men made the tea, O'Donnell still misbehaving, but sufficiently in check. Now she was back. I had visions of outraged virtue. Drugged men wrestling and lurching through the pajama party. What would they tell their fierce, social mothers? Were they terrified? Was Susan crushed? Rhona was calm and casual. "Oh, they're doing fine. Having pillow fights and listening to rock-and-roll. They're only worried about when we'll make them turn off the record player."

Ah, the calm, sure voice of the British empire. "Righto! Good show! Well done! Now let's have tea."

First Sex Trip

Massachusetts, 1960

> This is another trip that takes place in Harvard Professor Leary's Newton Center home. This one is with jazz trumpeter Maynard Ferguson, his wife, Flora Lu, and Leary's then-girlfriend Malaca.
> —Editor

After we took psilocybin, I sat on the couch in Flora Lu's Elysian chamber, letting my right cerebral hemisphere slowly open up to direct sensual reception. Flora Lu and Maynard started teaching me eroticism—the yoga of attention. Each moment was examined for sensual possibility. The delicious grace of moving one's hand, not as part of a learned survival experience, but for kinesthetic joy.

I was wearing the silk shirt and velvet trousers that Flora Lu, true to her promise to be my fashion coordinator, had left on my bed while I showered. Flora Lu was wearing light blue silk. Maynard was a Florentine noble garbed in tight-fitting velvet pants. In a Moroccan caftan, Malaca was soft, touchable.

A fire burned gently in the hearth. The air was scented with incense.

With his sensitive ears now as big as the Arecibo dish, Maynard swayed with pleasure. Flora Lu floated around the room, her face transfigured with delight. Malaca blossomed into a flower of great beauty, her classic features now stylized with the dignity of an Egyptian frieze.

My eyes connected with hers. We rose as one and walked to the sun porch. She turned, came to me, entwined her arms around my neck.

We were two sea creatures. The mating process in this universe began with the fusion of moist lips producing a soft-electric rapture that irradiated the entire body. We found no problem maneuvering the limbs, tentacles and delightful protuberances with which we were miraculously equipped in the transparent honey-liquid, zero-gravity atmosphere that surrounded, bathed, and sustained us.

This was my first sexual experience under the influence of psychedelics. It startled me to learn that in addition to being instruments of philosophic revelation, mystical unity and evolutionary insight, psychedelic drugs were powerful aphrodisiacs.

Malaca was upstairs taking a bubble bath. Maynard dozed on the sofa. I stood by the glass doors in the dawn, aware that my sunrise-watching index had risen dramatically since initiating this research into brain-change.

Flora Lu floated around the room, her face transfigured with delight. Malaca blossomed into a flower of great beauty, her classic features now stylized with the dignity of an Egyptian frieze.

Flora Lu carried in a tray containing a silver coffee pot, a silver pitcher of cream, two porcelain cups, and bowl of apples, bananas, and shiny green grapes.

She placed the tray on a low table and rode gravity down to a sitting position on the rug. "I want to continue the discussion we were having last night."

I felt a flush of warmth in my body, as my face muscles softened into a smile. "Yes, I remember. The secret-of-the-universe business."

We had been sitting harmoniously in front of the fire when Flora Lu leaned toward me. "It's all sex, don't you see?"

It had all become clear. I saw... black jazz combos playing the boogie. Swedish blondes disrobing on a tropical beach. Tanned slim Israeli boys belly dancing to frenzied drums. A wizened, wrinkled old Chinese Madame smoked her opium pipe and smiled. Lazy water currents sloughed and the Ageless Crocodile by the cash register who managed the action, stirred slowly and sank a bit lower in the embracing muck. I heard soft laughter from dark corners and behind bushes.

FIRST PRISON TRIP
1961

> One of Leary's students at Harvard proposes an experiment during which psilocybin will be shared with prisoners. The idea is that there would be a measurable result—the rate of recidivism—and that would prove that the drugs were good psychological medicine. When the research project couldn't get cooperation through the Harvard administration, Leary made arrangements with the prison administration on his own and the experiment went forward. This is Leary's first trip in prison, as a psychologist turning on prisoners. Later, he would take a few trips using illicit psychedelics in prison as a prisoner, although he never reported on the specifics of any of those experiences.—*Editor*

And it happened that on March 27, 1961, in the large ward room in the prison infirmary in Concord, Massachusetts, five prisoners and three Harvard psychologists met for a trip. In the morning I was to turn-on with three of the convicts, and the two other prisoners and two graduate students would act as observers. Then in the afternoon Gunther Weil and Ralph Metzner and the two observing prisoners were to take the drug, and the rest of us were to act as guides. We brought a record player, tape recorder, and some books of classical art with us. Otherwise the room was bleak in decor, with four beds, a large table, and a few chairs. At 9:35 in the morning the bowl of pills was placed in the center of the table. I was the first one to turn-on in the prison project. I reached over and took fourteen milligrams of psilocybin. Then I handed the bowl to the prisoner next to me, and he took twenty milligrams and passed it on to the guy next to him who took twenty, and then next man took his. Then we pushed the bowl to the middle of the table and sat back to see what would happen.

I'll never forget that morning. After about half an hour, I could feel the effect coming up, the loosening of symbolic reality, the feeling of humming pressure and space voyage inside my head, the sharp, brilliant, brutal intensification of all the senses. Every cell and every sense organ was humming with charged electricity. I felt *terrible*. What a place to be on a gray morning! In a dingy room in a grim penitentiary, out of my mind. I looked over at the man next to me, a Polish embezzler from Worcester, Massachusetts. I could see him so clearly. I could see every pore in his face, every blemish, the hairs in his nose, the incredible green-yellow enamel of the decay in his teeth, the wet glistening of his frightened eyes. I could see every hair in his head, as though each was as big as an oak tree. What a confrontation! What am I doing here, out of my mind, with this strange mosaic-celled animal-prisoner-criminal?

I could feel the effect coming up, the loosening of symbolic reality.

I said to him with a weak grin, "How are you doing, John?" He said, "I feel fine." Then he paused for a minute and asked, "How are you doing, Doc?" I was about to say in a reassuring psychological tone that I felt fine, but I couldn't, so I said, "I feel lousy." John drew back his purple-pink lips, showed his green-yellow teeth in a sickly grin, and said, "What's the matter, Doc? Why you feel lousy?" I looked with my two microscopic retina lenses into his eyes. I could see every line; yellow spider webs; red network of veins gleaming out at me. I said, "John, I'm afraid of you." His eyes got bigger, then he began to laugh. I could look inside his mouth, swollen red tissues, gums, tongue, throat. I was prepared to be swallowed. Then I heard him say, "Well that's funny, Doc, 'cause I'm afraid of you." We were both smiling at this point, leaning forward. "Doc," he said, "Why are you afraid of me?" I said, "I'm afraid of you, John, because you're a criminal." He nodded. I said, "John, why are you afraid of me?" He said, "I'm afraid of you, Doc, because you're a mad scientist." Then our retinas locked and I slid down into the tunnel of his eyes, and I could feel him walking around in my skull and we both began to laugh. And there it was, that dark moment of fear and distrust, which could have changed in a second to become hatred and terror. But we made the connection. The flicker in the dark. Suddenly, the sun came out in the room and I felt great and I knew he did too.

We had passed that moment of crisis, but as the minutes slowly ticked on, the grimness of our situation kept coming back in microscopic clarity. There were the four of us, turned-on, every sense vibrating, pulsating with messages, two billion years of cellular wisdom, but what could we do trapped within the four walls of a gray hospital room, barred inside a maximum security prison?

Then, one of the great lessons in my psychedelic training took place. One of the turned-on prisoners was Willy, a negro from Texas, a jazz saxophone player and heroin addict. He looked around with his two huge balls of ocular white, shook his head, staggered over to the record player, and put on a record. It was a Sonny Rollins record, which he'd especially asked us to bring. Then he lay down on the cot and closed his eyes. The rest of us sat by the table while metal air from the yellow saxophone spinning across copper electric wires bounced off the walls of the room. There was a long silence. Then we heard Willy moaning softly and moving restlessly on the couch. I turned and looked at him and said, "Willy, are you all right?" There was apprehension in my voice. Everyone in the room swung his head anxiously to look and listen for the answer. Willy lifted his head, gave a big grin, and said, "Man, am I all right? I'm in heaven and I can't believe it! Here I am in heaven, man, and I'm stoned out of my mind, and I'm swinging like I've never been before and it's all happening in prison, and you ask me man, am I all right. What a laugh!" And then he laughed, and we all laughed, and suddenly we were all high and happy and chuckling at what we had done: Bringing music and love, beauty, serenity and fun, and the seed of life into that grim and dreary prison.

The session went on and on. There were high points and low points, ecstasies and terrors. My friend John, the Polish man, got sick and vomited. We all got pretty thoughtful. Why are there prisons? Why do some men put the warm cellular envelopes of their fellow men in metal cages?

THE BURROUGHS TRIP

Morocco, 1961

In 1961–62, Leary and beat poet Allen Ginsberg went around turning on various artists and poets to psilocybin—Robert Lowell, Charles Mingus, and Arthur Koestler were among the recipients. The longest trip—in the traditional sense of the word—involved a trek to Morocco to share the drug with William S. Burroughs.

Burroughs would denounce Leary's Psilocybin Project in a passage in *The Soft Machine*. But by the 1970s, the two men would be friends, perhaps because they had similar ideas about the necessity for deconditioning humans from programmatical thoughts and behaviors—and they also shared the idea that the future of humanity is in space—a fairly unusual view in bohemian circles.

Here's a fragment from Leary's report on the psilocybin trip in Morocco. They were also joined on the journey by Gregory Corso and Alan Ansen.—*Editor*

It was decided to pick up Burroughs and then go down to visit the fair. When we got to Burroughs' house, Allen Ginsberg walked around to the side and climbed part way up the wall and uttered his ritual greeting: Bill BUH-rows! Bill BUH-rows!

We waited by the door and after a minute it slowly creaked open and there, almost collapsed against the wall, was Bill. His face was haggard and tense, staring out like a man caught in the power of Sammy the Butcher. He reached his left hand over his sweating face. "Tried to slip out eyes of white-hot crab creatures."

"Bill, how are you doing?" "They gave me large dose. I would like to sound a word of warning. I'm not feeling too well. I was struck by juxtaposition of purple fire mushroomed from the Pain Banks. Urgent Warning. I think I'll stay here in shriveling envelopes of larval flesh. I'm going to take some apomorphine. One of the nastiest cases ever processed by this department.

"You fellows go down to the fair and see film and brain waves tuning in on soulless insect people. Minutes to go. Whew! The hallucinogen drugs bottle and smoke pictures, my dears. Compassion. Compassion. Beautiful and ugly spirits blossom in the brain. Too bad. Minutes to go. What can we do? Compassion brings no relief? See you at the fair." The door closed around him glowing metal lattice in purple and blue. He's the most resilient man in Hassan I Sabbah's mountain troop. He'll be all right. Good ol' Bill. He takes no prisoners.

First Acid Trip

Massachusetts, 1961

Michael Hollingshed was very eager for me to take LSD, but I resisted the idea. Everything I had heard about lysergic acid sounded ominous to me. The mushrooms and peyote had grown naturally in the ground and had been used for thousands of years in wise Indian cultures. LSD, on the other hand, was a laboratory product that had quickly fallen into the hands of doctors and psychiatrists. Then, too, I was scared. The sacred mushrooms were my familiar territory. I had them harnessed up to my brand of revelation and ecstasy. It was obvious that the more powerful LSD swept you far beyond the tender wisdom of psilocybin. Like everyone else, I was both fascinated and frightened by the lysergic lore.

Michael invited me one night up to his bedroom and took from his dresser a mayonnaise jar packed with the moist sugar paste. "There it is," he said. "The key to miracle and meaning. When are you going to take it?" I shook my head. "I'm having trouble enough understanding the sacred mushrooms. Sometime I'll take your LSD, but I'm not ready now." He laughed. "Psilocybin, the child's toy of the Indians. After you've taken LSD you'll view psilocybin as I do. Take a triple dose and watch television. Change the black and white to color."

In early December, Maynard and Flo Ferguson came up for the weekend. Maynard was playing in a Boston dance hall. It was an easy, pleasant weekend. Flo did beautiful things around the house and Maynard told funny stories about the band business. I had made it a rule that there was to be no grass smoking in the house and they would leave with Michael and turn-on while driving around the neighborhood. They were planning to leave for New York about five o'clock on Sunday afternoon. We were sitting in front of the fireplace, in the living room, and Michael was telling LSD stories. Flo and Maynard's interest perked up. The next thing I knew Michael was bounding downstairs with the mayonnaise jar and a spoon. A tablespoon, I noticed, overflowing. I was listening to records and not paying too much attention, until after about half an hour I looked up and I saw that Maynard and Flo were gone from this world, into some sort of trance. They were sitting on the sofa motionless, their eyes closed. But I could feel energy emanating from their bodies. I turned down the volume on the record player and sat watching them. After about fifteen minutes Flo opened her eyes and she laughed. It was not a nervous or a funny laugh. It was the chuckle of someone who was dead and gone and sitting on some heavenly mountaintop and looking down at the two billion years of evolution the way you'd look at a transient episode in a children's playground.

She looked at me and began to talk. It was pure *advaita Vedanta*. She was Krishna, lecturing Arjuna. She was reciting, in chuckling, hip Manhattanese, the essence of Hindu philosophy: Maya, nonduality, reincarnation. And this, mind you, coming from little Flo Ferguson, who hadn't finished high school and had never read a philosophy book in her life. She thought Indians wore headdresses and feathers. Now from her smiling rosebud lips was pouring the most powerful religious statement I had ever heard in my life. "Timothy, you've got to take this. Man, it's the beginning and the end. You've got to take it."

I looked over and Michael was observing me, carefully, with a smile on his face. He raised his eyebrows and shrugged. *"Well?"* I looked at Maynard. He was glowing quietly, smiling and nodding.

"I guess this is the time, Michael," I said. With quick bounds he was out of the room, and I could hear his tennis shoes rippling up the stairs, and he returned with the mayonnaise jar, and the tablespoon heaped to overflowing with the sugar paste. George Litwin, just about to leave to go home to supper, was sitting next to me. Michael glanced at him. He nodded, *"Why not?"* and took his spoonful.

> ## With microscopic clarity, I saw the egocentricity, the sham of my devoted-father routine. Is it too late, can I come back, glorify this rare trembling opportunity?

It took about a half-hour to hit, and then it came, sudden and irresistible. An endless deep swampy marsh on some other planet teeming and steaming with energy and life, and in the swamp an enormous tree whose roots were buried miles down and whose branches were foliated out miles high and miles wide. And then this tree, like a cosmic vacuum cleaner, went, "Ssssuuuck," and every cell in my body was swept into the root, twigs, branches, and leaves of this tree. Tumbling and spinning, down the soft fibrous avenues to some central point which was just light. Just light, but not just light. It was the center of life. A burning, dazzling, throbbing, radiant core, pure pulsing, exulting light. An endless flame that contained everything sound, touch, cell, seed, sense, soul, sleep, glory, glorifying,

God, the hard eye of God. Merged with this pulsing flame it was possible to look out and see and participate in the entire cosmic drama. Past and future. All forms, all structures, all organisms, all events, were illusory, television productions pulsing out from the central eye. Everything that I had ever experienced and read about was bubble-dancing before me like a nineteenth-century Vaudeville show. My illusions, the comic costumes, the strange ever-changing stage props of trees and bodies and theater sets. All spinning out from the momentary parts of the central God-eye-heart-penis-light.

After several billion years I found myself on my feet moving through a puppet show. Where does Timothy Leary belong in this dance of illusion? I thought of my kids and walked somehow upstairs to the second-floor landing and opened the door to my daughter's room. Susan was sitting in bed, the classic thirteen-year-old with her hair up in curlers, frowning in concentration at the schoolbook in her lap, while rock-and-roll music blasted through the room. It was pure *Saturday Evening Post* cover Americana. The puppet doll teen-ager glanced up. "Hi, Dad." She was biting a pencil and looking at the book. I slumped against the wall, looking with amazement at this marionette stranger, from assembly-line America. She glanced up again, quickly. "Hi, Dad, what would you like for Christmas?" She went on biting the pencil, frowning at the book, waving slightly at the beat of the music. In a minute she looked up again. "Hi, Dad, I love you."

A shock of terror convulsed me. This was my daughter and this was the father-daughter game. A shallow, superficial, stereotyped, meaningless exchange of Hi, Dad, Hi, Sue, How are you Dad? How's school? What do you want for Christmas? Have you done your homework? The plastic doll father and the plastic doll daughter both mounted on little wheels, rolling by each other around and around on fixed tracks. A complete vulgarization of the real situation—two incredibly complex, trillion-cell clusters rooted in an eternity of evolution, sharing for a flicker this space-time coordinate. And offered this rare chance to merge souls and bring out the divinity in the other, but desiccated and deadened into the Hi Dad Hi Susan squeaks.

I looked at her beseechingly, straining for real contact. I was stunned with guilt.

With microscopic clarity, I saw the egocentricity, the sham of my devoted-father routine. Is it too late, can I come back, glorify this rare trembling opportunity? I turned and slowly walked downstairs to the front hallway. Eleven-year-old Jack sat on the floor watching television. I sat down next to him. Without taking his eyes from the tube he said, "Hi, Dad. Great program, Dad." Once again the piercing realization of my blind misuse of this divine Buddha child.

I followed his gaze to the television set. Jack Benny, wise, noble, long-suffering guru, was going through a routine about death, the transience of life. Memories from my boyhood—Fred Allen, Jack Pearl, Will Rogers, Charlie Chaplin. Each week the cosmic television show repeating the same message, infusing into the frail, karmic forms of Benny, Allen, Rogers, the ancient messages, comic and tragic. Don't you see? It's spinning by you, blinding you. Don't you catch on? You're going, you're going. Use the few seconds that remain.

I suddenly knew that everything is a message from the impersonal, relentless, infinite, divine intelligence, weaving a new web of life each second, bombarding us with a message. Don't you see! You're nothing! Wake up! Glorify me! Join me!

Then there were three men on the TV screen. One was in a barber's chair, one was facing him, the other had his back turned. The third man suddenly wheeled around and said, looking straight through the television tube, into my eyes, "You've been dead for two seconds." [Laugh track laughter]

The cosmic playwright uses diverse messengers to get the point across. It's in a flower; it's in the light of a star that takes millions of years to reach your eyes. Sometimes for the stupid he even writes it out in words in a television drama, for those whose obtuseness can only be opened up by the boob tube. I'd been dead for two seconds. And this is what hell is like. I could look back over the past forty years with chagrin, with pain at my blindness. Every second presented me with a golden chance to tune in, to break through, to glorify, to really groove and dance with God's great song. And every second of every minute of every hour of every day I grimly played out my narrow little mental chess game. The action was still continuing on the television set, but my consciousness was shrieking in remorse. Agonbite of inwit! Waste! Waste! Fool! How many times had I heard the message? In all the great religious books, in all the poems, everyplace it confronted me. Forget yourself. Tune in on the big picture.

Then I heard music. I looked up at the screen and saw Doris Day leaning towards me, her hands beckoning. What was she singing? "The second time around, I'm so glad I met you, the second time around." It suddenly dawned on me, that's what death is, that's what hell is. It just keeps going, there's no end to it. You have your first chance to touch and taste, tissue, direct contact with God's energy, and then when that's over, a second time, you repeat the whole process, but it's different. There's a plastic film between you and the divine process around you, your egocentricity, your deadening mind has created a plastic hell. That's the meaning of ghosts and anguished spirits, doomed for eternity to exist, separated from life, that precious, fragile gift that we squander every second of this so-called mortal reality. The second time around. Second time, it's the carbon copy. One little interval out of step. This time you are one vibration beat behind that ecstatic intersection which the living call life and which the tormented call paradise.

Later, I swam into the kitchen. There was a book on the table. I flipped it open. In a second I saw the history of every word on the page tracing back, back, back, back, to the beginnings of written language. Back down to one sentence—the death of the father, *morte du pere,* and in that sentence, boiled and bubbled down to the essence of the one word, *morte,* there it was again, the grim confrontation.

I sat on the kitchen floor, looking at my body, my skin of delicately treated leather, exquisitely carved but dead. I saw plastic veins, blue and pink, and I saw celluloid fingernails. My mind was spinning like a computer that had no connection with anything live—no flesh, no cell, no sweat, no smell. I had lost my senses, *morte*. Death. With only the mind to spin out its universe of thoughts. Now you know what hell is. The mind cut off from the body, from life, from seed, from cell.

George Litwin staggered into the room. He was now a nineteenth-century Frenchman: Cocky, carefree, courageous. He swung around and looked at me with anguished eyes. We were both dead men, trapped in the doomed submarine. We said nothing, but our eyes met in sympathetic terror. Gone, gone. It's finished.

It was straight telepathic communication. I was in his mind, he was in my mind, we both saw the whole thing, the illusion, the artifice, the flimsy game-nature of the mental universe. The popeyed look of terror changed to mellow resignation and the Buddha smiled. He murmured the word, "Harvard," smiling.

I said, "America." He said, "Duty." And I said, "Love."

He flinched and then nodded, smiling sadly, Yes, love. That was the ultimate confrontation. The last shattered secret from the Buddha bag. It's all an illusion, even love. And what's left? The wise, cool, all-seeing eyes and the slight smile around the mouth. Acceptance, peace, resigned serenity. It's all in your own mind, baby, the whole bit from beginning to end. It is the spinning out of your own chessboard. Caesar, Alexander, Christ, America, Timothy Leary, George Litwin, even love—they only exist because you think them. Stop thinking them and they do not exist.

> It was straight telepathic communication. I was in his mind, he was in my mind, we both saw the whole thing, the illusion, the artifice, the flimsy game-nature of the mental universe. The popeyed look of terror changed to mellow resignation and the Buddha smiled.

Then George was gone. I floated to the door. Perhaps outside the house I could find something solid, real, tangible.

I ran out to the lawn, snow, trees, starlight. It had never been more beautiful. Etched, sharp, magnified. I stood there, listening for the answer. Where is the center? What is real? What can we do?

Then rapidly, but completely, in careful detail I recapitulated the social and intellectual history of the human race. I relived and worked through every solution that the human mind had attempted. Society, migrations, groupings, tribal wanderings, invasions, the planting of crops, the building of cities, the restless searching for possibility and meaning, the moral codes, the taboos and kinships, the emergence of stumbling species groping for answer, for order, for center, the lost mutants trapped in their forebrains, trying to think and act their way back to the center. What to do and where to go? I could foresee the outcome of any action I should begin.

And slowly, like a string being reeled back, I retraced my steps to that central spot in front of the fire where the session had begun. Here was the beginning. Michael, the master trickster, sitting silently and waiting. Maynard and Flo on the couch. Flo draped across Maynard's lap. I said something. Flo sat up and replied. Maynard's head went back and laughed. Then I repeated the same message, Flo sat up, Maynard laughed. I repeated the same message. Flo sat up and Maynard laughed. We were trapped in a time loop. Doomed forever to repeat a brief television commercial, over and over again at the station break.

Flo and Maynard were beautiful, stage-dressed, made-up characters. The classic frail beauty, and the dapper young musician, costumed for their parts.

I looked at Michael. His sad face bore the record of all human suffering. He was clearly one of the twelve apostles, cast for the moment in the funny little drama of Michael and Cambridge, come to teach us the ancient message that the center is back by the fire with your friends. Quiet detached trust and mutual acceptance of the ultimate cosmological horror. Limited. Limited. Limited. Trapped in our nervous systems, struggling to catch one glimpse every decade or two of the ancient cellular membrane meaning of life. Waiting patiently through those long periods of plastic isolation, until that next vibrant contact came.

> The latticework shuttling of energy patterns. All forms, all structure, man-made and organic, were seen clearly in their molecular and particle nature.

George, by this time, had disappeared. His ordeal of death and renewal ran along a similar line, with only the stage props different. At that moment of ultimate confrontation he knew that his place was at home with his wife. He ran to his car and with conscious, accurate reflexes started it and drove down the street. Ahead of him was a Volkswagen and behind with their lights gleaming were three cars, except that George was really in a *troika* fleeing across a snowy Russian steppe. In front of him, bouncing along, was a rabbit. And behind him, yellow eyes gleaming with pursuit, were three wolves. Over and over the snow they sped, the rabbit, the *troika*, and the pursuing wolves, till suddenly the lights flashed red in front of him. Dutifully the rabbit stopped, George reined up his *troika*, and in ballet rhythm the three wolves, poised on their haunches, waited patiently. Then the light flashed green, and off they went again, the rabbit, the *troika*, and the straining wolves. George knew that distance had to be kept or there would be danger for the rabbit or danger from the wolves. When his street loomed up he automatically swung to the right, parked the car, ran to the house, and buried his head in his wife's lap for the rest of the evening, which was the beginning of their next voyage.

Meanwhile, my cosmic odyssey went on and on. One myth after another, lived out and traced back to the basic flash in the silent, impersonal, whirring of primal vibrations, beyond sense, beyond cell, beyond seed, beyond life. The latticework shuttling of energy patterns. All forms, all structure, man-made and organic, were seen clearly in their molecular and particle nature. All structure was an illusion. Every form was a momentary stage prop for the great theater of illusion, continually changing.

My previous psychedelic sessions with psilocybin had opened me up to the sensory levels of consciousness, pushed consciousness out to the membrane frontier, contact points of eyeball and light, ear canal and sound. Psilocybin had sucked me down into nerve nets, into the somatic organs, heart pulse, and air breath; had let me spiral down the DNA ladder of evolution to the beginning of life on this planet. But LSD was something different. Michael's heaping spoonful had flipped consciousness out beyond life into the whirling dance of pure energy, where nothing existed except whirring vibrations, and each illusory form was simply a different frequency.

It was the most shattering experience of my life. I sat there, a part of Einstein's equation, seeing it all, terrified and confused, desperately looking for some structure which would last against the ruthless bombardment of energy waves, and through it all, sitting with his head cradled in his knees, was the architect of enlightenment, the magician, who had flicked the switch to this alchemical show of revelation. Michael, the trickster.

As I watched him, looking for an answer in his face, he changed. No longer the cool, cynical Buddha eye, I now saw him as the lost victim of the revelations he'd unleashed. As I studied him carefully I could see scars on his face and hands and even threads of antennae sticking up from his skull.

He shot a piteous, resigned look in my direction. He is the victim of some greater power; his consciousness has been captured, perhaps by intelligences from another planet. He is not a free agent. He knows what he's doing but he has no control over it. His turning us on is not an act of love and glorification but some sort of compulsion. He *has* to do it. He wants us to share the immobilization of his profound vision, to share his celestial dilemma. His cosmic loneliness. How can one act when one sees that all form is an illusory package of vibrations, just like your television screen? Nothing but beams of light while we comfort ourselves with childish explanations of philosophy and religion.

The effects of the drug began to wear off by dawn. I was still higher than I had ever been before, but at least some structure was coming back. The flow of vibrations had stopped, and I felt myself freezing into a mold of plastic. There was a terrible sense of loss, of nostalgia, for the long hours, eons really, when one was at the heart of meaning and the radiant core of the energy process.

I walked up to the Fergusons' room. They were sitting transfixed, feeling the same despair at their ejection from paradise. I knelt before Flo with my head in her lap, tears came down her eyes, and I found myself shaking with sobs. Why had we lost it? Why were we being reborn? In these silly leather bodies with these trivial little chessboard minds? For the rest of the morning I was in a daze, stunned by what had happened, trying to figure out what to do with these new revelations, how they make sense, what to do with life routines, which were obviously pointless, senseless, and completely artificial.

First Isolation Trip

Millbrook, New York 1964 (written 1983)

By 1964, Dr. Leary had left Harvard amidst scandal for playing a bit too loose and free with the experimental stash—helped along by what he called "a mild kick." By 1964, he was America's first and only full-time psychedelic spokesperson, living with friends and family in a mansion donated by wealthy patrons in Millbrook, New York, an upstate town about an hour north of New York City. At Millbrook, Leary and his crew of explorers tried various tactics and techniques for experimenting with consciousness, both with and without psychedelic drugs.

—*Editor*

On March 21, the vernal equinox, we celebrated a pagan festival, burning the gigantic pile of brush, listening to the furious hiss of green wood, watching the red fire flicker on our faces. Then we assembled in the tennis house, now renamed Meditation House, sitting in a candlelit circle while Alan Watts consulted the *I Ching*. Watts, whose orientation was past and Eastern rather than scientific and Western, used the *I Ching* as an elegant mumbo-jumbo tea ceremony, which raised the aesthetic level of our gathering and made us feel part of an ancient tradition.

We lit the fireplace. I took a large dose of Heavenly Blue acid, and silently, one by one, the company left. Our new plan called for each member of the community to spend one week in silence and solitude in the Meditation House. Meals would be brought three times a day and left on the stone terrace. "The voyager" would write notes for any special request.

This was my first trip without guide or companion. I spent the first night totally beyond my mind, spinning back through the evolutionary past, time traveling into the future, reliving many genetic states. When I opened my eyes, there I was, back again.

I walked outside and howled at the moon. I listened with animal wisdom to the sounds of forest life, looked up at the Big House, watched lights in bedrooms winking out, felt love and empathy for the residents.

I watched the sun rise, wandered for hours around the estate, followed brooks babbling springtime, broke through thickets to discover a glorious hidden lake shimmering with the promise of summer. Then there were breathtaking meetings with deer herds, foxes trailing red fur along the green. I spent a long time lying on a hillside, bundled in my heavy coat, watching the play of life around me, listening to the gossip of trees, insect and animals, discovering that there is one biological intelligence that expresses herself through the various living forms.

The flow of vibrations had stopped, and I felt myself freezing into a mold of plastic.

Everything was alive, pulsing. Everything connected. In the wrong context this perception can be horrible: everything is alive? And connected? Nightmare! But in nature the perfection of the universe was undeniable.

I was beginning to understand dimly the enormity of the spectrum of vocabularies used by organisms to communicate with each other. In this timeless environment, hypersensitive to the signals from my memory banks and my chattering hormones, and altered by commands from DNA control templates cunningly buried in my cells, I recognized that everything was information. Everything was shouting, "Hey, look at me, I'm here. Open up, I have a message." Trees waved their slender limbs in invitation. Flowers winked. The sun drenched me with stellar information fresh from the solar oven. Every time I breathed, in came millions of airborne organisms, each squirming with DNA network news. Everything I put in my mouth—the spoon, a swallow of water, every bite of food, every sexy-smooth lick—contaminated me with data.

I began to speculate that everything we absorb, including neurological stimuli such as sounds, words, gestures from others, creates antibodies, enabling others to become permanent parts of us. I sought to be corrupted, i.e, broken to pieces, by others' biological and neurological signals. For the rest of the solitary week, I read, made notes, walked, tripped.

At sunset on the seventh day, Easter Sunday, the doors of the Meditation House were rolled open, and the community assembled for a reunion. The leather-covered log book in which I had entered my notes was turned over to the next searcher, chosen by lot, and I returned to the routines of the planet.

First Techno-Media Trip

Hollywood, 1967

> While hanging out in L.A. in 1967, film Director Otto Preminger asked Leary to come to his home to consult for a film Preminger was making.—*Editor*

At this point who should pop in but film director Otto Preminger, seeking information about LSD for a movie, *Skidoo*. He asked me many questions about the effects of LSD, and I queried him about filmmaking. A week later I dropped by Otto's luxurious Manhattan townhouse, where the cunning director persuaded me to run an LSD session for him. It was another one of those life-changers for me—coming from three years in romantic Arcadia to Otto's plastic-fantastic, white-and-chrome, futuristic projection room which bristled with dials, lights, levers, and other control-panel paraphernalia.

There was no fireplace. No candles!

As soon as the acid kicked in, Otto sprang into manic action. He turned on the TV—sacrilege! You were supposed to go within, float down your cerebral aqueduct, paddle by the Isles of Langerhans, skirt the Sylvan fissure, and wash up blissfully on the shores of your frontal lobes chanting "Om Sweet Om." Not Otto. His shiny, hairless head had turned into a space helmet and he was high as an orbiting com-sat as he dialed and turned ever-changing realities, deliberately disrupting focus and color.

I tried to find a slow repetitious Ravi Shankar record that would spin us within. No luck. His collection was all movie scores. Otto now had two more TV sets switched on. He stared with gleeful satisfaction at a screen flickering with random patterns of dots. Then I realized that Otto was demonstrating something important to me. As a movie director Otto took on the godly task of inventing a reality—he selected plot, location, actors. He externalized his vision on film and marketed it so that millions of human beings could inhabit his creation. I realized the great shapers of human destiny were those who had accepted this role, who had dared to impose their version of reality upon others. All successful philosophers and mythmakers have been able to persuade others to live in worlds that their minds have invented.

Watching Otto's accelerated brain in action jolted me out of the nostalgic-pastoral phase. At Millbrook we had been living in a timewarp. Avoiding technology, we got close to nature and to the wise-sensual animal places in the brain. But Otto's electronic technology could extend the brain and liberate us from the muscular. Millbrook was a pleasant but repetitious feudal drill. The next stage in evolution, my own at least, was going to involve information and communication. I resolved on the spot to move to Hollywood and learn how realities were produced and directed.

First High Dose Exiles On Acid Trip, With Rosemary Leary

Algeria, 1971

> What a difference a few years make, when those years are the late 1960s. By 1971, Leary had been in various prisons for possession of small amounts of marijuana. He had escaped prison with the assistance of the radical left guerrilla group, the Weather Underground. He was in exile in Algeria, where he was staying in an uneasy alliance with exiled members of the Black Panther Party led by author and Panther legend Eldridge Cleaver. In this passage, he and his wife, Rosemary, have trekked to a spot in the Algerian desert and taken a massive, walloping dose of LSD.—*Editor*

After the customary preparations, we plunged outward, cutting a pathway of law through the tumbling chaos of interplanetary time. We were dropping—dropping through layers of pluriverses in a barely controlled escape curve. Soon we must give the order to slow down and halt on one level. We had no idea which one to choose. In the vast multiverse we're all merely scattered seeds—seeds that must survive many elements if we are to grow. In four-dimensional space it appeared as solid. From time one could see universes separated from one another by layers. The universes remained unknown to one another, unrealizing they were each part of a composite structure of fantastic complexity. We decided that the next universe, irrespective of what it was, should be the one to enter. Our brains were computing madly the data pouring in. First reports indicated that this new galaxy was scarcely different from our own. We weren't surprised. Each layer of the multiverse differs only slightly from the next.

We touched down on a planet of purity. The land was pure gold, sky pure blue. And that was all. We had found the intersection of form and substance. Coming in from time so rapidly required a certain effort in order to center attention on only one plane. As soon as we relaxed, we felt the absolute pleasure of dwelling on all planes simultaneously. We existed in a place where the air was jeweled and faceted, glistening and alive with myriad colors, flashing, scintillating, and beautiful.

> Sand creates itself. Each grain a uniform cutting crystal blown against cliffs, wearing down mountains, chiseling away promontories of individuality hurled by the waves against the coast.

She appeared in Her Divine Radiance, manifesting several images simultaneously, each containing a different combination of colors. It was as if She looked out through a series of tinted, opaque masks covering Her body and interweaving on either side. The image that I took to be the original lay slightly to one side of the multiple image and in better focus than the rest. She smiled and asked, "Have we become one entity?"

"No. It is simply that existing on the multiversal level, in Time, we are capable of linking neurologies to form a powerful single unit."

On an ocean of sand. Where does it come from?

Sand creates itself. Each grain a uniform cutting crystal blown against cliffs, wearing down mountains, chiseling away promontories of individuality hurled by the waves against the coast.

Sand is an addictive substance. Grab handfuls and drip paint with it. Bas-relief. Build castles, forts, an empire. It's a truth drug. Time's simple message. Draw diagrams. Formulas. Write the one great simple truth. In sand. Love letters in the sand.

I placed my hand on it. Sahara sable is finer than sea sand. Fingers sifted into the warmth. It became firmer, harder, moister, cold. We swelter in desert sun, while inches below there is a wet cold world.

"It's all desert," she laughed.

Suddenly he came: El Arabi, god of the desert. His message registered in the mind as sound, but the ears claimed to have heard nothing. Several thousand years of memory tape. Thirst. Heat. Oasis. Possession. Treachery. Suspicion. Hospitality. Skin hungers for soft oils and perfumes. Ear thirsts for sound of splashing liquid. Watching the stars. Fierce struggle to survive. Harsh. Loyalty. Treachery. Blood on the sand. Sperm on the sand. Sandstorm.

We could look through sand and see a valley of vegetation now covered up by the relentless engulfing grasp of sand. Sand is cancer eating up earth. Mountains of sand crushing down on life. Pressure creating oil. Sand is essence of mineral. Oil is essence of current human life. Sand is the worst enemy of machine. Oil lubricates. The contest of mineral vs. biological imperative.

'Which side do you root for?"

She laughed. We drank a mouthful of water from the flask and knew what that meant. It was out of our hands.

I walked out into the desert and felt lonely beyond human contact. I looked back to proton center. She was sitting on the Mound of Venus. I leaped back up sculptured footprints. We lit a smoke. She inhaled deeply and held smoke letting eyes and cheeks bulge comic.

The wind blew against our backs softly. We could feel it. Then hear it. Then see it rippling the sand. The sun was setting and from down below we heard the cry of shepherd calling flocks down from the mountain. We packed the pillow cases and folded the rug. Walking down we understood about the veil.

First Ski Trip On Acid

Switzerland, 1972

> After escaping America's prison, the Learys found that they also had to escape Eldridge Cleaver, who put them under

"house arrest" in Algeria for not following Cleaver's restrictive rules. Leary eventually finds himself in Switzerland under the protection of a wealthy outlaw and con artist named Michel Huachard. While there, Leary learns how to ski.

Clue: Delta V is an astrodynamic term that Leary used, somewhat imaginatively, to represent the idea of a psychedelic adept—or more frequently a psychedelic couple—that is able to operate at high velocity and rapidly change trajectory.—*Editor*

The ski satori, the velocity revelation….

The Professor strains through novice exercises for three weeks. At the beginning his muscles are weak from unaccustomed movements. He is on the slopes from ten until five every day, but progress is slow. For fifty years his gross musculature had been programmed to deal with the pull of gravity without swinging his hips.

He watched the Swiss three-year-olds, brought to the slopes on weekends by parents. Sliding along with confidence, being trained to ski at the time when nervous systems can easily learn anti-gravity maneuvers.

After three weeks of straining he apparently senses that the time has come to reimprint. After loosening his conditioned patterns and suspending imprints by means of Neurological Techniques developed in the research laboratories at Harvard University (i.e. 500 micrograms of LSD), he finds himself standing on skis at slope top, brain disconnected from body and laryngeal muscles of the mind. Bathing, as it were, in Waves of Energy.

The faster you go, the more control you have and the easier it is to maneuver!

Craig, standing next to him, waves and plummets down the slope. Without hesitation, the Professor opens the door to his body, climbs in, turns the dial and follows, imitating every movement of his guru. Freed from mind and habit, the Body is a simple vehicle to operate. One points the skis downhill and slides the contours of the slope. The terrain does the thinking. Slight changes in direction are accomplished by shifting the weight and swinging the mid-section.

The faster you go, the more control you have and the easier it is to maneuver! There is little to do except surf the swift gravity wave. To make sharp turns you skid both skis until they point in the new direction. But this must be done at the highest possible speed. Slowing down is yielding control to gravity's grasp.

Craig, glancing back, sees his wild-eyed pupil, laughs, and keeps going. They soar down the expert slope, miles of curving, twisting descent, and skid in a shower of snow to the bottom.

Craig lifts his poles in exultation. "You have broken through. You can ski."

"It is a moment of Neurological Revelation," he shouts. "Like the First Fuck." He motions to the lift-bar. Once again. Faster. He can't wait to get to the summit. Standing on the crest he shouts his discovery. "The faster you go, the safer you are!"

He pulls back the sleeve of his jacket to check his watch. "Let's time it. Faster."

Freed from mind and habit, the Body is a simple vehicle to operate.

For the next two hours the Fugitive rides his body down the run marveling at rushing pleasure. Like the first acid experience. High-speed philosophy. All-out kinesthetic yoga. Before cracking this hedonic gap, skiing, like adolescent sex, had been inefficient groping work. Two minutes to descend twenty feet, straining, pushing skis against slippery snow, leaning on poles, anxiously studying each yard of surface, struggling to keep control, to go slow. Total larval concentration on which muscles to be pulled, which angle to be wrestled. The satisfaction came in remaining erect, unharmed.

Now he flashed through two kilometers in two minutes. Ice patches, formerly terrors to be avoided are now accelerators to be shot through. Moguls are now round energy clusters to be used as turn curves. What had been feared is now used to increase intensity and control. The snow-covered mountain is an anti-gravity energy-apparatus bristling with knobby dials to select, direct, modulate, amplify the wind-swift current.

The sun has set. Craig and the Professor stand at the summit looking down at the Rhone Valley and the orange clouds. There are no other skiers left, only the restaurant staff bundling into the last cable car down. The wind whips the unprotected peak.

"I hate to leave," he says.

"We're always the last ones to come down."

They plunge down the right side of the valley wall, skid around the left turn throwing up waves of snow, dive straight to the base of the high T-bar lift, veer right bumping through the steep mogul field, thread down the narrow, icy roadway, slash a sudden right-angle down a wide, steep meadow, slide right again, burst under the tow cable out to the top of the mid-slope, and race, hunching low, poles tucked under armpits, wind ripping their faces.

At the bottom station they reach down to snap off bindings, swing skis over shoulder and, suddenly earthbound, clumsily roll in ski-boot, high-gravity gait along the village streets to the saloon. They stack the skis outside and open the door to a rush of warm air scented with alcohol, smoke, perfume and the steam of healthy bodies. The atmosphere has that soft-electricity of congenial, happy, sophisticated people who like themselves and each other.

They order beers and sit back, content.

"It's addictive."

Craig smiles in agreement. "It's neurological yoga. It's muscular meditation. It does everything that the oriental gurus claim, but it's more."

"The danger bit is fascinating," says the Philosopher. "The risk buzz."

"Power freed for pleasure and clean speed," says Craig. "I'm glad you got the hit today. It's happened for you and you can never lose it. It's very sexual." He motions to the saloon filled with hi-fi people. "It's new, you know, like a mutation. High-speed skiing has just developed in the last twenty years. It's part of what's happening all around. Electronics and computers and jet planes and space travel. It's the same principle and it's the exact opposite of what we learned in the old life. It's the paradox of technological civilization. The faster you go the more control you have. Like the pilot flying 700 miles per hour with fingertip control. On the ground you need a tow-tractor to make the plane turn."

"You go up and you come down."

"And a lot can happen up there. Sometimes you don't come down with whom you went up. You move with those at the same velocity."

"Delta V."

* * * * *

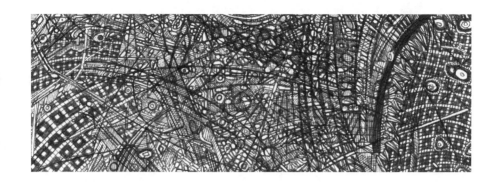

Chapter Two
VISIONS

Presented here are some of the more poetic and visionary passages taken from Dr. Leary's various trip experiences.

—*Editor*

1965

In the beginning was the turn on. The flash, the illumination. The electrictrip. The sudden bolt of energy that starts the new system.

It was the flash that exploded the galaxies, from which all energy flows. It was the spark that ignites in the mysterious welding of amino-acid strands that creates the humming vine of organic life. It is the brilliant neurological glare that illuminates the shadows of man's mind. The God-intoxicated revelation. The Divine union. The vision of harmony, samadhi, satori, ecstasy which we now call psychedelic.

What happens when you turn on? You close your eyes and the thirteen billion-cell brain computer flashes multiple kaleidoscopic messages. Symbolic thought merges with sensory explosions, fusing with somatic-tissue events; ideas combine with memories personal, cellular, and evolutionary; embryonic thoughts collapse into molecular patterns.

You open your eyes and you see your tidy television-studio world of labeled stage props fusing with sensory, somatic, cellular, molecular flashes.

The Light shineth in the darkness and the darkness comprehendeth it not.

The turn on bolt shatters structure. Reveals the frozen nature of the artificial stage-set men call reality. Certitude collapses. There is nothing but the energy which lights every WoMan that comes into the world. $E = MC^2$.

We discover that we are not television actors born onto the American stage set of a commercially-sponsored program twenty centuries old. We are two-billion-year-old carriers of the Light, born not just of blood nor of the will of the flesh, nor of the will of man, but of the Light that flashed in the Precambrian mud, the Light made flesh.

First Trip—Psilocybin Mushroom Visions
1960

pomposity of scholars
impudence of the mind
smug naiveté of words
If Whiskers (the cat) could only see!
Stagger in hahahouse. Roaring. Into bedroom.
Fahahalling on bed
Doubled in laughahafter.

Deterring follow, watch curiously, maybe scared.
Then
Dettering begins to lafhahahaf.
Yes, he laughs too.

You see, Dickohoho? The impudent mind?
Comedy? Yes.

Old Dettering floats over
sea-toad face
bloated
purple green warts
froggy
We stand looking down over
allgreen grass blade leaf petal in

focus sharp clear shining
changing waves color
like floodlight slides
at summer dance hall
kaleidoscope

In Mandy's arms
Her body warm foam rubber
Marshmallow flesh
My body gone
Fallen into her
Two leafy water plants
Twined together, undulating warm Bermuda sea
deep
Entangled so that no one
Not even plants themselves can tell
Which leaf
Which stem
Belongs to which.

Gone again, gone into
Palace by Nile
Temple near Hong Kong
Babylonian boudoir, Bedouin pleasure tent
Gem-flash jewel
Woven color silk gown movement
Mosaics flaming color Mezzo emerald Burma rubies
Ceylon sapphire
Mosaics lighted from within glowing, moving,
changing.
Hundred reptiles, Jewel encrusted.
Hammered Moorish patterned
Snakeskin.
Snake mosaic, reptiles piled in
Giant, mile-square chest
Slide, slither, tumble down central
drain

One

Gerhart and Joan on next bed laughing
Next to me mermaid, laughing.
Put hand on hip where
Skin pokes through bikini lacings
Hand up soft back until fingers
Sink in quicksand of flesh through skin through ribs
Closed eyes
Moving belts like
Inlaid Moorish patterns

Plummeting back through time,
snake time,
fish time
Down through giant jungle palm time,
greeny lacy ferny leaf time.
Watching first life oozing,
writhing,
twisting up.
Watching first sea thing crawl to shore
Lie with her. Sand-rasp under cheek
Then float sea-thing, down
Deep green sea dark
I am first living
Thing I
Am

Lying ecstatic eyes closed on a Triassic-Jurassic
sedentary rock formation, one hand on Mandy's
vertebrae hearing interstellar voices
from the Mexican patio, light years away. Voice calls.
Where are you? Here! I am lying unicelled looking up up up
through the spiral unfolding of two billion years,
seeing it all ahead of me, ovum, segmentation,
differentiation of organs, plant, fish, mammal,

monkey, baby, grammar school, college, Harvard,
Mexico, Cuernavaca. They want me way up there.
Is it worth the whole journey? To start
the two-billion-year cycle once again? No. Why bother?
Let's move over to the Precambrian sludge,
no too wet, abysses, overlying waters,
narrow littoral rocks,
let's try that Cenozoic snaky jungle.

* * * * *

SYNTHETIC MUSHROOMS

Morocco, 1961

We roll like diamond hoops down to the waterfront. The electricians had outdone themselves. Sidewalks emblazoned with Arabic script. What's that jeweled object? Gem box sparkled, lived. Once, for a long moment, that translucent fairy tower is a glowing turquoise blue. For one moment and then the combination shatters into a million bursting fragments of color: blue, red, green, yellow. No color, no possible shade of color, is missing from that silent, flaming explosion. What is it? Oh, an empty cigarette package in the gutter's lambent fire. Come along. Oh, see the conquering art of Moorish slave girls crowned with diadems. What a happy crowd! Dancing with lively, mocking sound, blue tattoos on forehead.

Happy night walking to the fair with Baudelaire. This world of stone and metal; brittle and bright. The family of the King picked their way across daintily. Flasks of perfume, fabrics lamé and spangled, rich furnishings of brocade and gold, and we haven't even arrived at the gate to the fair yet. Tickets. Industrial exhibits of the Alien Species. Alan Ansen and Gregory Corso are smiling. Delights of Islam.

We slide through canvas slit in Arab tent, Ginsberg guiding, to watch the dancing. Oh, the endless chanting. Behind us a girl nurses her baby. Boy dancers sway and rock drunkenly. Chanting. And become dust that is scattered on the desert wind, swinging circles clashing bronze cymbals. Ansen, eyes closed, sways back and forth to the beat. The foremost shall be brought nigh unto God in the Gardens of Delight. The cymbals laughed and chanting told the secret. On inlaid couches they recline face to face. Four Moorish soldiers, tender young in the front row, eyes popping in wonder, while immortal youths go around them with goblets and flagons and a chalice of wine. The dance endless. Exactly. Timeless. The cadenced rise and fall of breathing rhythm. Up.

Down. Up. Down. Around us veiled women, mysterious, soft, inviting, and fruit according to their choice and flesh of fowls that they desire. Ginsberg is whispering that the color of the robe meant a different tribe. Rifs from the mountains. Fountains? Can't hear his talk of... Berbers? Proud? Loud? Joyce? The chanting river roar mounts. There too are Houris, with dark eyes like hidden pearls. Entire families leaning forward to watch, robed, listening, nor are they bemused. Ginsberg whispers they're all high on pot or hashish. That's why the dance goes so long, endless and always flowing. *Yeaaaaaaaah.* But they hear the ayeing peace. Peace. Now the Gnaowanian drummers leap on stage: whirling, pounding the deep, heavy drums. Each beat quivers, energy coils, we become each beat. Amid clustered plantains and spreading shade and gushing water. The drummers, Negroid, fierce, laughing. High too? Moors use water in their architecture because to a desert people the splashing sound and rippling sight of fountains is the highest delight. The dance tempo quickens to a Niagara chaos of sound and high-raised couches. Consorts have we created and we have made them virgins. On low stairs leading up to the stage a Moorish maid beams out curious, flirting look from olive slits behind a gray veil, utterly loving and perfectly matched we have made them. I fell in love with veiled eyes.

LSD VISIONS

1961

She was an insect-queen buried deep in the damp tunnels of the anthill humming with genetic energy and you burrowed down dark to find her. She was a bird of plumage trembling in the thicket for your feathered embrace. She was a taxi-dancer from Alexandria.

He wandered around murmuring ecstatically about his new insights into space, time, meaning. She lay by the fire with her arms over her head murmuring his name. When he ignored her, her soft eyes moved around the room and her body twisted in search. She looked at me and smiled. Then she unfolded and swam towards me. Her husband was standing looking out the window. Her husband. His wife. Now she was all-woman receptive earth; tomorrow she would be reincarnated as a pretty graduate student. I retreated behind the couch.

DMT Visions

1962

Minute 1: soft humming noise . . . eyes closed . . . suddenly, as if someone touched a button, the static darkness of retina is illuminated . . . enormous toy-jewel-clock factory, Santa Claus workshop . . . not impersonal or engineered, but jolly, comic, lighthearted. The dance of the body, humming with energy, billions of variegated forms spinning, clicking through their appointed rounds in the smooth ballet . . . .

Minute 2: open eyes . . . there squatting next to me are two magnificent insects . . . skin burnished, glowing metallic, with hammered jewels inlaid . . . richly costumed researchers, they looked at me sweetly . . . dear, radiant Venusian crickets . . . one has a pad in his lap and is holding out a gem-encrusted box with undulating trapezoidal glowing sections . . . questioning look . . . incredible . . . and next to him Mrs. Diamond Cricket softly slides into a latticework of vibrations . . . Dr. Ruby-emerald Cricket smiles.

Minute 3: Body . . . I am swimming in tissue tidelands . . . body consciousness . . . thanks for the chance to be the dance . . . infinity of life forms . . . funny exotic energy nets . . .

Minute 4: Spinning out in the tapestry of space comes the voice from down below . . . dear kindly earth-voice . . . earth station calling . . . where are you? . . . what a joke . . . how to answer . . . I am in the bubbling beaker of the cosmic alchemist . . . no, no softly falling stardust exploding in the branches of the stellar ivory birch tree . . . what? Open eyes . . . oh dear lapidary insect friends . . . beautiful orange lobsters watching me gently . . . faces shattered into stained-glass mosaic . . . Dr. Tiffany Lobster holds out the casket of trapezoidal sections . . . look at glowing key . . . where is Venusian ecstasy key? . . . where is key for the stellar explosion of the year 3000?

Minute 5: . . . my body begins to disintegrate . . . flow out into the river of evolution . . . goodbye . . . gone star space in orgasm pulses of particle motion . . . release . . . flashing light, light, light. . . .

Minute 6: Earth voice calling . . . you there, meson hurtling in nuclear orbit . . . incorporate . . . trap the streaking energy particle . . .

slow down . . . freeze into body structure . . . return . . . with flick of open eye the nuclear dance suddenly skids into static form . . . see two clusters of electrons shimmering . . . the energy dance caught momentarily in friendly robot form . . . hello . . . next to them a candle flame . . . center of million-armed web of light beams . . . the room is caught in a lattice of light-energy . . . shimmering . . . finger taps molecular . . . molecular . . . Ah yes . . . *MOLECULAR!*

Eyes closed but after-image of candle flame remains . . . eyeballs trapped in orbit around internal light center . . . celestial radiance from the light center . . . light of sun . . . all life is frail filament of light . . .

Minute 7: heart of the sun's hydrogen explosion . . . our globe is light's globe . . . open eyes drape curtain over sun flare . . . open eyes bring blindness . . . shut off internal radiance . . . see Chiaroscuro God holding a shadow box . . .

Keep eyes open . . . whole room, flowered walls, cushions, candle, human forms all vibrating . . . all waves having no form . . . terrible stillness . . . just silent energy flow . . . if you move you will shatter the pattern . . . all remembered forms, meanings, identities meaningless . . . gone . . . pitiless emanation of physical waves . . . television impulses crackling across an interstellar grid . . . our sun one point on astrophysical television screen . . . our galaxy tiny cluster of points on one corner of TV screen . . . the ten-billion-year cycle of our universe is a millisecond flash of light on the cosmic screen flowing endlessly with images . . . .

*****

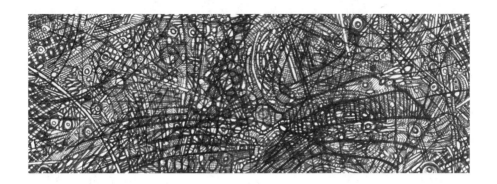

Chapter Three
THEORIES & REFLECTIONS

THE NATURE AND PURPOSE OF PSYCHEDELIC EXPERIENCES
1965

Visionary plants (the peyote cactus, the divine mushrooms of Mexico; divinatory vines and roots) have been used for thousands of years. Today's technology provides synthetics of the active ingredients of these ancient and venerable concoctions. These foods and drugs produce ecstasy, the most sought after and most dreaded experience known to man. Ex-stasis [ecstasy] means, literally, out of, or released from a fixed or unmoving condition. Some theorists like to suppose a steady growth in human consciousness; others, especially Eastern philosophers, point to alternating cycles of expansion and contraction and warn that man's awareness may contract down to the robot-narrow precision of certain overorganized species of life. The anthill and the computer remind us that increased efficiency does not necessarily mean expanded awareness. I believe psychedelic drugs and their effects should be viewed in the context of the emergent philosophy of the evolution of intelligence.

The Renaissance-Reformation mythos would have us believe man is the chosen lord of all species. But in the last few decades, scientific instrumentation has confronted man with visions, vistas, and processes that have thoroughly dissipated any philosophic securities. Astronomers speak of billions of light years; physicists of critical nuclear-process structures that last only microseconds. Genetic blueprinting strands are so compact that the seed of every human being on earth today could be contained in a box 1/8 inch on a side. New scientific data define man as an animal only dimly aware of the energies and wisdom surrounding and radiating through her.

We can use our *rational* faculties to change our instruments and language; to invent new mathematics and symbols to deal with processes beyond our neurological scope. But then comes neurological implosion. Rational consciousness is a fragile, tissue-thin artifact, easily blown away by the slightest alteration of biochemistry, or by the simplest external stimulation—for example, by a few microvolts strategically introduced into specific areas of the brain, or by the removal of *accustomed* stimulation.

The potential of cerebral association is of the order of thirteen billion to the twenty-five-thousandth power per second. But, we think rationally at a maximum rate of three concepts or ten phonemes per second. Our present mental machinery cannot possibly handle the whirling, speed-of-light, trackless processes of our brain—the organ of *consciousness itself.*

The paradox: to use our heads—to push out beyond words, space-time categories, social identifications, models and concepts—it becomes necessary to go out of our generally rational minds. If we at times seem uncertain, too ready to spin out unproven hypotheses, this is a sign of the preliminary, rapidly changing speculation that inevitably characterizes a new breakthrough in the realm of ideas.

That our research provokes fierce controversy suggests that man's accepted view of himself is coming into collision with new concepts.

THE STABLE WORLD THAT USED TO BE

It is useful to see all cultural institutions as expressions of the epoch's basic mythos; each discipline simply reorchestrating underlying themes of the age. What fails to fit the mythic harmonic tends to be heard as disruptive dissonance. Thomas S. Kuhn describes how scientific activities are determined by paradigm—a distinctive world view, defining the problems and methods of any era. Science cannot go beyond the paradigm's limits without risking being seen as eccentric, even "unscientific." During the last fifty years our basic world view seems to have been undergoing another of these gigantic struggles of ideologies of which the current controversy over psychedelic drugs is but a minor skirmish. The older, classic world view concerns itself with equilibria among forces that are visible, external, predictable, measurable, manageable by man, within the realm of macroscopic consciousness. The religious expression of this mythos is Protestantism, with its emphasis on behavior, achievement, balancing, and rationality. Democracy, communism, parliamentarianism, all emphasize the macroscopic, visible aspects of behavior. Classic physical science emphasized the orderly; God, the master engineer, balancing the clockwork equilibrium of material forces. But the metaphorical interpretations we impose betray our implicit, basic (usually unconscious) commitments: God runs the universe the way a good Christian runs his business; the way Andrew Mellon ran the country. Like a factory.

Psychology again fits the dimensions of the myth. Behaviorism (a scientific movement invented and manned by Protestants) recognizes only visible actions. Human personality is pictured as ruled by conservation principles—ego, id, superego pushing toward equilibrium. There was much more to Freud than this; but the Hasidic, expansive, and mystical aspects of Freud's thinking have not survived the post-Freudian Protestantization of the theory.

THE EMERGENT-ROOT MYTH

Evidence from every branch of science testifies to energies and structures which, though fantastically potent, are microscopic—indeed, invisible. The good old macroscopic world is a rather clumsy, robotlike level of conception. Structure becomes process. Matter becomes a transient state of energy. Stasis becomes ex-stasis.

The same exponential mythos appears in other institutions. Overproduction, overkilling, industrial pollution, remind us that older economic, political, religious, artistic, psychological views of man, defined in externals and behaviorals, are reaching an agonizing end-point.

Psychology, man's view of his nature, is always the last to adapt a new world view. From the standpoint of established values, the psychedelic process is dangerous and insane—a deliberate psychotization, a suicidal undoing of the equilibrium man should be striving for. With its internal, invisible, indescribable phenomena, the psychedelic experience is incomprehensible to a rational, achievement-oriented, conformist philosophy. But to one ready to experience the exponential view of the universe, psychedelic experience is exquisitely effective preparation for the inundation of data and problems to come.

Each of us possesses around 30 billion brain cells, several times the number of human beings in the world. Each brain cell is a computer capable of relating with as many as 25,000 others. The number of possible associations is of the order of 30 billion to the twenty-five-thousandth power, a quantity larger than the number of atoms in the universe. This electrical-chemical complexity is the anatomical structure of consciousness.

Something like 100 million sensations pour into the brain each second. The brain itself fires off around five billion signals a second. Yet we are aware of only the millionth fraction of our own cortical signaling. Huge areas of the brain (neurologists call them "silent areas") are blocked off from consciousness. Reflective neurologists pose disturbing questions: ". . . has man, perhaps, more brain than he knows what to do with? Is his huge 'neo-pallium' like a powerful engine in a decrepit automobile that can never utilize more than a fraction of the available horsepower?"

IMPRINTING AND RE-IMPRINTING

Little is known about the learning processes by which the brain's enormous potential is limited and contracted. According to psychologist Clifford Morgan, Konrad Lorenz happened to be present when some goose eggs in an incubator hatched. For this reason he was the first large moving object the goslings saw. Much to his surprise, the goslings began following him about as though he were their parent. The young goslings, in fact, would have nothing to do with their mother goose and insisted on his constant company. This learning takes place very rapidly and without any specific reward. . . . The imprinting phenomenon . . . can take place only during a short interval (a few hours or a day or two) and at a certain time (usually shortly following birth). It also seems irreversible; difficult to alter through subsequent learning. However, some true learning may be connected with it. Young goslings, for example, at first follow any human being who has been the first object contact after hatching. A few days later, however, they learn the individual characteristics of the person who ordinarily leads them to food and shelter, and then they will follow no one else. Thus imprinting may be a natural stage in maturation.

Here is a sudden irreversible learning, which seems independent of motivation, reward, conditioning—a sudden, shuttle-like fixing of the nervous system. Once taken, the picture then determines the scope and type of subsequent "lawful learning." Imprinting, a biochemical event, sets up the chessboard upon which slow, step-by-step conditioning takes place.

One awesome aspect of imprinting is its unpredictable, accidental quality. In another experiment, young birds were presented with a Ping-Pong ball at the critical moment and spent their remaining lives pursuing plastic globes. This amusing and frightening experiment reminds us that each of us perceives the world through biochemical-neurological structures accidentally laid down in our earliest moments. We may be chasing the particular Ping-Pong ball which, at those sensitive moments, has been imprinted on our cortical film.

Certain alkaloid molecules (psychedelic drugs) dramatically suspend the conditioned, learned aspects of the nervous system. Suddenly released from its conditioned patterning, consciousness is flung into a flashing loom of unlearned imagery, an eerie, novel landscape where everything seems possible and nothing remains fixed. Might we consider the psychedelic effect as a temporary suspension of imprinting?

Some current neurological research already indicates that serotonin is a key factor in the transmission of nerve impulses. There is a difference in serotonin metabolism between infants and adults and between "normal" and schizophrenic persons. LSD also affects serotonin metabolism. Marplan, a drug, "builds up the brain's stockpile of serotonin," has a tranquilizing effect on mental patients, and blocks the action of LSD.

Serotonin might contribute to the imprinting process necessary for "normal" perception. The shifting, unfixed imagery of the involuntary (and unpleasant) psychotic state, and the voluntary (ecstatic) psychedelic state, are associated with a change in the body's serotonin level. Psychedelic drugs may provide the possibility of reimprinting—a neurological restatement of the "death-rebirth" experience so often reported during psychedelic moments: during the psychedelic session, the subject's nervous system is in a disorganized flux closely analogous to that of infancy. And here we come to the accelerated personality change, rapid learning, and sudden life changes so regularly reported by psychedelic researchers.

THE PSYCHOLOGICAL SITUATION

A most confusing aspect of psychedelic drug phenomena is the wide variation of responses. There is the common factor of going beyond the imprinted, learned structure, but the specific content of what comes next is always different. LSD, mescaline, and psilocybin simply do not produce a generally predictable sequence of responses.

Psychedelic substances have negligible somatic effects. Their site of action is the higher nervous system. Once "normal" modes of awareness are suspended, specific consciousness changes occur due to set and setting.

Set refers to what the subject brings to the situation, his earlier imprinting, learning, emotional and rational predilections, and, perhaps most important, his immediate expectations about the drug experience. Setting refers to the social, physical, emotional milieu of the session.

Most important is the behavior, understanding, and empathy of the persons who first administer the drug and who remain with the taker while the drug is in effect. The psychedelic controversy itself is a broad social confirmation of the set-setting hypothesis. The extreme suggestibility, the heightened vulnerability to internal or external stimuli which leads some to paranoia, others to cosmic ecstasy, points to the critical importance of expectation and environmental pressure.

THE PROBLEM OF COMMUNICATION

Words are inadequate to describe the speed, breadth, and shuttling flow of a 30-billion-cell cerebral computer and the fears aroused by the very nature of the topic. Not long ago I spent an afternoon with Dr. Richard Alpert and Dr. Ralph Metzner, lecturing to the staff of The Hudson Institute, one of the country's most respected think tanks. About thirty-five scientists were present, and in closing the meeting, the chairman—a well-known physicist who had taken LSD several times—questioned the possibility of verbal communication about the psychedelic experience: "Those who have taken a psychedelic drug realize it can't be talked about, and those who haven't naively assume that it can be talked about with the current vocabulary."

After the meeting, we met with four members of the institute who had had previous experience with psychedelic drugs. Three were strangers, but without any social niceties, these men immediately plunged into a frank, avuncular coaching process, as though Alpert, Metzner, and I were rookie pitchers being instructed by four veterans; as though all seven of us were meeting to figure how to explain to earthlings the procedures and events of our totally different world.

Each coach had a different strategy. One said we should make our psychedelic lectures completely personal: "Tell, concretely, what happened to you." "Nonsense," said another. "Be strictly objective and scientific. Rely only on published data." A third disagreed: "Make it practical. Tell the audience about the dosage, how long it lasts, what people say and do during sessions." The fourth was the most psychological: "Recognize the fears of the listener. Anticipate his objections. Be humble. Stress the dangers and problems. Don't put him on the defensive."

But all four advisors were unanimous in criticizing my central metaphor: " 'You have to go out of your mind to use your head,' is guaranteed to scare rational, intellectual people. Use a positive, familiar, psychological jargon. Talk about creative reorganization or perceptual reintegration."

But psychedelic drugs do take us beyond our normal conceptual framework. Most of the great religions have taken this disturbing goal of ex-stasis as their central program.

FEAR OF THE POTENTIAL

Experienced psychedelic veterans recognize certain fears generated by the psychedelic process:

> **1. Cognitive:** loss of rational control; fear of disorientation and confusion.
> **2. Social:** doing something shameful or ludicrous; the loss of social inhibitions.
> **3. Psychological:** self-discovery; finding out something about yourself that you do not want to face.
> **4. Cultural:** discovering the painful truth about the institutions with which one is identified; seeing through the tribal shams; becoming disillusioned with one's social commitments and thus becoming irresponsible.
> **5. Ontological addiction:** finding a new dimension of experience too pleasant; perhaps all men share the hunch that normal consciousness is a form of sleepwalking and that somewhere there exists a form of "awakeness" from which one would not want to return.

This fear of losing the social-ego identity is based on an illusion. One who has the courage to undergo the shattering of the illusion will die, but only in the mystical sense, "so that he may live again." A Zen koan says: "Be dead, thoroughly dead, and do as you will." The healing process, which Paul Tillich describes as "taking a walk through hell," brings the transcendence that lies beyond.

Like other forms of anxiety, these five fears are related to deep yearnings and potentials. For each terror, there is a corresponding liberation. Terror is a negative desire. The terror of seeing yourself is the negative aspect of the ecstasy of really seeing yourself.

What Happens on LSD?

Playboy, 1966

What happens to almost everyone is the experience of incredible acceleration and intensification of all senses and of all mental processes. This can be very confusing if you're not prepared for it. Around a thousand million signals fire off in your brain every second; during any second in an LSD session, you find yourself tuned in on thousands of these messages that, ordinarily, you don't register consciously. And you may be getting an incredible number of simultaneous messages from different parts of your body. Since you're not used to this, it can lead to incredible ecstasy or it can lead to confusion. Some people are freaked by this niagara of sensory input. Instead of having just one or two or three things happening in tidy sequence, you're suddenly flooded by hundreds of lights and colors and sensations and images, and you can get quite lost.

You will often sense a strange, powerful force beginning to unloose and radiate through your body. In normal perception, we are aware of static symbols. But as the LSD effect takes hold, everything begins to move, and this relentless, impersonal, slowly swelling movement will continue through the several hours of the session. It's as though for all of your normal waking life you have been caught in a still photograph, in an awkward, stereotyped posture; suddenly the show comes alive, balloons out to several dimensions and becomes irradiated with color and energy.

The first thing you notice is an incredible enhancement of sensory awareness. Take the sense of sight. LSD vision is to normal vision as normal vision is to the picture on a badly tuned television set. Under LSD, it's as though you have microscopes up to your eyes, in which you see jewel-like, radiant details of anything your eye falls upon. You are really seeing for the first time not static, symbolic perception of learned things, but patterns of light bouncing off the objects around you and hurtling at the speed of light into the mosaic of rods and cones in the retina of your eye. Everything seems alive. Everything is alive, beaming diamond-bright light waves into your retina.

Your nerve cells are aware—as Professor Einstein was aware—that all matter, all structure, is pulsating energy. There is a shattering moment in the deep psychedelic session when your body, and the world around you, dissolves into shimmering latticeworks of pulsating white waves, into silent, subcellular worlds of shuttling energy. But this phenomenon is nothing new. It's been reported by mystics and visionaries throughout the last 4000 years of recorded history as "the white light" or the "dance of energy." Suddenly you realize that everything you thought of as reality or even as life itself, including your body, is just a dance of particles.

When you sit across the room from a woman during an LSD session, you're aware of thousands of penetrating chemical messages floating from her through the air into your sensory center: a symphony of a thousand odors that all of us exude at every moment: the shampoo she uses, her perfume, her sweat, the exhaust and discharge from her digestive system, her sexual aroma, the fragrance of her clothing—grenades of eroticism are exploding in the olfactory cells.

Touch becomes electric as well as erotic. I remember a moment during one session in which my wife leaned over and lightly touched the palm of my hand with her finger. Immediately a hundred thousand end cells in my hand exploded in soft orgasm. Ecstatic energies pulsated up my arms and rocketed into my brain, where another hundred thousand cells softly exploded in pure, delicate pleasure. The distance between my wife's finger and the palm of my hand was about 50 miles of space, filled with cotton candy, infiltrated with thousands of silver wires hurtling energy back and forth. Wave after wave of exquisite energy pulsed from her finger. Wave upon wave of ethereal tissue rapture, delicate, shuddering, coursed back and forth from her finger to my palm.

Your nerve cells are aware—as Professor Einstein was aware—that all matter, all structure, is pulsating energy

Sex under LSD becomes miraculously enhanced and intensified. I don't mean that it simply generates genital energy. It doesn't automatically produce a longer erection. Rather, it increases your sensitivity a thousand percent. Let me put it this way: Compared with sex under LSD, the way you've been making love—no matter how ecstatic the pleasure you think you get from it—is like making love to a dummy in a department-store-window. In sensory and cellular communion on LSD, you may spend a half hour making love with eyeballs, another half hour making love with breath. As you spin through a thousand sensory and cellular organic changes, she does, too. Ordinarily, sexual communication involves one's own chemicals, pressure and interactions of a very localized nature in what the psychologists call the "erogenous zones." A vulgar, dirty concept, I think. When you're making love under LSD, it's as though every cell in your body—*and you have trillions*—is making love with every cell in her body. Your hand doesn't caress her skin but sinks down into and merges with ancient dynamos of ecstasy within her. That is what the LSD experience is all about. Merging, yielding, flowing, union, communion. It's *all* lovemaking. You make love with candlelight, with sound waves from a record player, with a bowl of fruit on the table, with the trees. You're in pulsating harmony with all the energy around you.

I remember a session a few years ago in which, with horror and ecstasy, I opened my eyes and looked into the eyes of my wife and was pulled into the deep blue pools of her being floating softly in the center of her mind, experiencing everything that she was experiencing, knowing every thought that she had ever had. As my eyes were riveted to hers, her face began to melt and change. I saw her as a young girl, as a baby, as an old woman with gray hair and seamy, wrinkled face. I saw her as a witch, a Madonna, a nagging crone, a radiant queen, a Byzantine virgin, a tired, worldly-wise Oriental whore who had seen every sight of life repeated a thousand times. She was all women, all woman, the essence of female eyes smiling, quizzically, resignedly, devilishly, always inviting: "See me, hear me, join me, merge with me, keep the dance going."

IMPRINTING & REIMPRINTING WITH PSYCHEDELIC DRUGS

Western psychology recognizes no methods or possibilities for getting off the imprint board (unwanted, deeply embedded psychological fixes taken during particular moments of vulnerability during childhood and adolescence) and insists that we must stay with the survival compulsions that were accidentally imprinted by our random experiences.

But one can, at least temporarily, suspend an unwanted imprint with psychedelic drugs, and tune in on the internal and external energy accessible to the human nervous system.

Note again that the suspension of imprint is temporary. No one has yet demonstrated the possibility of remaining "high" indefinitely. The problem of re-entry, return to externals, must always be met. We can re-imprint carefully, selecting the new chessboard, choosing the persons and externals to which we will become voluntarily hooked.

Before the addicted "dope fiend" or alcoholic can be cured, he must recognize his affliction. Similarly, the first step in losing a habitual imprint is to recognize that our consciousness is totally hooked to certain externals, to recognize the limits and directions of our imprints. Some forms of psychoanalysis aim to do this. Long chains of associations are laboriously traced, step-by-step, to the original imprint situation. A new sequence of associations is attempted, centering on the person of the analyst (transference). But, as Freud saw, verbal interaction in the consulting room cannot duplicate the impact of the original biochemical structuring. Each external imprint is uniquely located in space and time.

If conditioning is building sand structures, imprinting is like stamped-out metal patterns.

The only way to rewire neural patterns is to interfere with the neurotransmitter sequence at the synapse, thus retracting the old imprint and allowing for a new imprinting. Shock, illness, trauma, drugs, child delivery, stimulus deprivation and electrical charge are the only ways to change the chemistry of the synapse. When action inside the body becomes overwhelmingly intense so as to alter synapse chemistry, the imprint life-lines to the external environment are retracted. The chance to re-imprint is offered.

Learning, conditioning and other educational or coercive methods of behavior-control that seek to change accidental imprint-based behaviors write their messages on sand. After each daily tide of association and reward-punishment, the associations must be repeated. The coercive nature of learned behavior is not clearly seen because it appears voluntary. Indeed, the conditioned robot is obsessively drawn back to his place in the sandbox. Larval civilization is a Beckett landscape. Every morning millions of humanoids rush to their sand-piles and re-construct them.

The ordeal of Sisyphus was an exciting heroic adventure compared to the monotony of social conditioning. The humanoid robot, operant-conditioned to symbols, is a reward addict. If we remove the symbol-rewarding environment, if we fail to produce the conditioned stimulus, the humanoid robot goes mad, because she has nothing to do.

We can accurately speak of stimulus junkies. If there is no sandbox and no sand to work on, there is panic. Social deprivation creates desperate reward hunger. The social reality of conditioned response requires continual rewarding. The prisoners continually rebuild their restricting reality walls which crumble if they are not continually reinforced.

The operant conditioning of behaviorists like B.F. Skinner is robotry and can exist only in a controlled, scheduled, coercive society.

If, to continue this rather gritty metaphor, conditioning is building sand structures, imprinting is like stamped-out metal patterns. Trying to re-condition an imprint taken in childhood with reward-punishment is like dropping single grains of sand on a forged steel pattern. Decades of sand can wear away the iron pattern. Senility can wear down the imprint. The aging politician gets lazy, the aging pedophile becomes too fatigued to hustle children. Etc.

To change the shape of metal forms one must apply energy sufficient to rearrange the patterning of molecules: change the electromagnetic field. So it is with neural imprints. Just as heat is used in metallurgy, so is it necessary to apply massive biochemical energy to loosen the molecular synaptic bonds. Internal stimuli drugs, trauma, illness, deprivation, and shock can retract the external neural life lines.

The initial, accidental, childhood imprint-fix is sudden. Post-imprint conditioning, however, takes time and repetition.

Just as heated metal hardens into the new form, so does the re-imprinted nervous system harden into new circuits, freeze back into new membrane forms. I speak here of psychedelic metallurgy—serial re-imprinting, the neurologic craft of recasting and recircuiting the bio-electric wiring.

With the present repertoire of psychedelic neurotransmitter drugs it is apparently only possible to re-imprint about once a week. You cannot re-imprint every day. It takes from five to seven days for the new-mind-mold to harden. LSD research indicates that it takes a retractory period of a week for the structure to build up.

It is a fundamental principle of exo-psychology *[ed: Leary's theory of brain evolution]* that conditioning centers around the positive and negative poles of the imprint. The initial, accidental, childhood imprint-fix is sudden. Post-imprint conditioning, however, takes time and repetition. Around the initial sexual imprint, for example, there builds up, over the years, billions of conditioned associations. This forms the structure of personality.

During a re-imprinting session it is probable that the new imprint includes the old conditioned structure. You re-imprint your spouse, for example. Where new models are imprinted, it is necessary to start building up new circles of conditioned reflexes around the new imprint. This takes time. Some early LSD researchers concluded that a six month waiting period should occur between LSD sessions. In psychological terms, to "work through the new insights." The exo-psychological phrase is "to allow new conditioning to network around the new imprints." But the new imprint model must be present during the re-conditioning.

Neurologic, therefore, requires that one plan one's re-imprinting sessions carefully so that those aspects of previous realities which one wishes to exist in the future reality are present to be imprinted and new models imprinted during the "sensitive" period remain around to allow new conditioned associations to build up around them.

Usually the person re-imprints the old conditioned stimuli.

One often hears the complaint from people who have taken LSD repeatedly that, after a while, the "trips" were the same. Such comments reveal a lack of knowledge of the re-imprinting process. If the recasting of the mind occurs over and over again in the same place with the same set of characters (usually one's larval egos) then the same neural form repeats. This is like having the most precise and expensive photographic equipment and, without moving it, continuing to photograph the same object.

A more thoughtful use of the recasting, reincarnative potentialities of the nervous system was exemplified by the two neurologicians, a newly married couple, who embarked on a psychedelic world tour. The first step was to purchase 'round-the-world air tickets which had to be used within one year. The couple then thought of themselves as orbiting satellites of the planet who had to accomplish the circumnavigation in twelve months.

The procedure was to fly to a country and to enquire as to the "spiritual" center of that nation. In Japan, they were told to go to Kyoto. In India, to Benares. In Greece, to Eleusis, etc. In Kyoto they asked where the spiritual center, the "soul" of Kyoto was to be found. They were given many suggestions and visited each center to pick up neuro-genetic vibrations. They spent a week reading about the history, politics, culture, art, myths of Japan and Kyoto. Then they went to the "holiest" place, ingested a strong, psychedelic chemical which suspended old imprints and opened the nervous system to new imprints which in this case were structured by the architecture and regalia of the Emperor's palace. For six hours they absorbed the signals of the place and became neurologically Japanesed.

This is the only way to "see the world"—to retract the imprint roots and move the unattached nervous system to a new locale to which the neural lines are extended.

Without such flexibility-vulnerability, we can experience nothing outside the membrane that was formed at the time of the last imprinting, which for males is the time of adolescence or, in the case of women, their last child-birth. Most world travelers move their robot-bodies from country to country experiencing only symbolic versions of their own home grounds.

Neural touring—as in the example of the couple above —is not an end in itself, but a rudimentary training exercise for neurologicians learning how to use the Einsteinian serial possibilities of the brain.

The Promises & Perils of the Rapture Circuit
1976

Positive, transcendent experiences on mild dose psychedelics, or even with cannabis, open up what I call the rapture circuit, in which the experimenter is temporarily liberated from their social games and concerns and gets to experience the brain as a pleasure organ.

This neurosomatic "Rapture Circuit" mediates body-time experience—sensory and somatic—registered by the external sense organs (optical, aural, tactile, taste, smell, temperature, pressure, pain, balance, kinesthetic) and signals from the internal somatic system (breathing, circulation, sex, ingestion, digestion, elimination). Until now, sense organs have served to provide cues for larval, hive-conditioned systems: "Red is for stop; green for go." The rapture imprint occurs the first time direct aesthetic impact is received, and "red" and "green" are seen as pulsating light energy. The eye does not "see things," but registers direct sensation uninterrupted by symbolic thinking. Intensity of sensation is dramatically increased, duration seems longer. Conditioned cues from larval circuits are not wiped out, but harmonized (often humorously) with the direct sensations. Consider the modes of meta-rational, polymorphous-erotic perception attained by Fechnerian introspectionists, Zen masters, artists, and marijuana adepts.

The existence of the natural rapture experience has always been a taboo topic proscribed by larval social law because it is instinctively recognized that if the human being discovers a source of pleasure and revelation within her body, the commitment and dedication to conventional social rewards will diminish. This is the genetic predisposition to escape from the social imprints. Historically, it is no accident that the aesthetic, rapturous experience was accepted by affluent aristocracies who are "above and beyond" social sanctions.

The transition from a life centered on social consensus reality and a life that privileges rapture is complicated because it has been viewed as anti-social. The perils of hedonism! The socially dangerous discovery of the rapture circuit is this: "My natural bodily sensations are more pleasurable and more interesting than territorial social rewards. I want to stay loose and high. Mundane affairs are robot."

During the 1960s both Presidents Johnson and Nixon clearly recognized that the American work-aesthetic was threatened by hedonism. While young men lost interest in fighting on far-flung foreign shores, ominous comparisons were made in State of the Union speeches to the "fall of the Roman Empire." The misguided implications were that Hedonism corrupted the Empire and, that if decadence could be checked, the Empire would continue expanding.

The static moralism of Johnson-Nixon fails to perceive the evolutionary cyclical nature of history. Just as blossom follows bud so does virtuous republic become centralized empire and empire flower into somatic hedonism. It is to slow this trend that the socialisms ban rock-and-roll.

In the past, hedonism invariably led to the collapse of empire. Imperial capture could not compete with private rapture. Hedonism has, therefore, not been recognized by larval historians as an evolutionary advance, but as a social threat. When the somatic nervous system can be attached to and detached from larval imprints at will, the first step away from imprinted-robothood has been taken. The enraptured brain begins to transceive directly the first language of nature—the metacultural biochemistry of the body. When the individual begins to attain control of neurosomatic function, and can dial and tune the pleasures of the body, she is taking the first step towards control of the nervous system.

The existence of the natural rapture experience has always been a taboo topic proscribed by larval social law.

The emergence of this Hedonic Psychology in the 1960s was greeted with official scorn and persecution. Larval politicians correctly saw the cultural perils of hedonism. The neurosomatic perspective frees the human from addiction to hive rewards (which are now seen as robot) and opens up vistas of natural satisfaction and meta-social aesthetic revelation. The revelation is this: "I can learn to control internal, somatic function, to select, dial, tune incoming stimuli, not on the basis of security, power, success, or social responsibility, but in terms of aesthetics and psychosomatic wisdom. To feel good. To escape from terrestrial pulls."

Since the neurological sixties, we have seen an efflorescence of consumer sensuality and body interest. Massage, sensory awakening, yoga, martial art, diet, health-food-fads, erotic performance. The "new hedonics" is a manifestation of the first beginnings of enraptured Zen Consciousness.

The triggering causative factor in this mutation was, of course, the discovery of neurosomatic drugs. In the 1960s people in technological societies discovered that neurosomatic chemicals "turn-on" the body and provide escape from mundane reality-islands. The moment of this discovery is, for most, an ethical detonation. Bodily revelation has been routinely condemned as immoral by every larval social-ethical system at the same time it has been eloquently praised by those aesthetes who have tuned into the somatic network. But the problem of neurosomatic rapture is that it is a post-larval reaction, and has mixed survival value for terrestrial existence.

Each survival imprint addicts the nervous system to certain external stimuli registered as, or associated with, "positives." Similar addiction occurs in the rapture circuit, where certain organs become "rapture prone," and certain aesthetically pleasing sounds, odors, tastes, touches, and somatic reactions become associated with hedonic reward. Rapture can become a satin trap, as the history of decadent leisure classes testifies. Decadence is repetitious indulgence, whereas true self-indulgence is intelligent, flexible, and evolving. Our terrestrial civilizations are over-populating the globe with insectoid social structures. Exactly at this point, a new generation asks the transcortical questions, "Why? What's next?"

The hedonistic neuro-somatic rapture answer is to "feel good." But the hippie philosophy, however appealing, soon became anti-evolutionary and regressive. The drop out philosophy produced an entire generation of bare-foot philosophers, discovering the joys, infantile delights of direct sensuality. History teaches us that the worship of play and display, eros and beauty, is a vulnerable phase, essentially incapable of protecting itself. Woodstock and the French Revolution both teach the lesson: evolve or perish.

How To Boot Up Your Brain
1994

The human brain, we are told, is a galaxy of over a hundred billion neurons, any two of which can organize and communicate as much complex information as a mainframe computer.

Many cognitive psychologists now see the brain as a universe of information processors. Our minds, according to this metaphor, serve as the software that programs the neural hardware (or wetware). Most of the classic psychological terms can now be redefined in terms of computer concepts. Cognitive functions like memory, forgetting, learning, creativity, and logical thinking are now studied as methods by which the mind forms "databases" and stores, processes, shuffles, and retrieves information.

Noncognitive functions such as emotions, moods, sensory perceptions, hallucinations, obsessions, phobias, altered states, possession-trance experiences, glossolalias, intoxications, visionary images, and psychedelic perspectives can now be viewed in terms of ROM brain circuits or autonomous-sympathetic-mid-brain sectors that are usually not accessed by left-brain or forebrain conscious decision. These nonlinear, unconscious areas can, as we well know, be activated intentionally or involuntarily by various means. The pop term "turn on" carries the fascinating cybernetic implication that one can selectively dial up or access brain sectors that process specific channels of information signals normally unavailable.

These concepts could emerge only in an electronic culture. The mystics and altered-state philosophers of the past, like the Buddha or St. John of the Cross or William James or Aldous Huxley, could not describe their visions and illuminations and ecstasies and enlightenments in terms of "turning on" electronic appliances.

I'm not advocating the naive assumption here that the brain is a computer. However, by using cybernetic terminology to describe mind and brain functions, we can add to our knowledge about the varieties of thought-processing experiences.

> ## This use of a manufactured artifact like the computer to help us understand internal biological processes seems to be a normal stage in the growth of human knowledge.

This use of a manufactured artifact like the computer to help us understand internal biological processes seems to be a normal stage in the growth of human knowledge. William Harvey's notions about the heart as a pump and the circulation of the blood obviously stemmed from hydraulic engineering. Our understanding of metabolism and nutrition inside the body had to await the science of thermodynamics and energy machines.

Two hundred years ago, before electrical appliances were commonplace, the brain was vaguely defined as an organ that secreted "thoughts" the way the heart processed blood and the lungs processed air. Forty-five years ago, my Psychology 1-A professors described the brain in terms of the most advanced information system available at the time—an enormous telephone exchange. This metaphor obviously did not lead to profitable experimentation, so the brain was generally ignored by psychology. The psychoanalytic theories of Freud were more useful and comprehensible, because they were based on familiar thermodynamic principles: neurosis was caused by the blocking or repression of surging, steamy, over-heated dynamic instincts that exploded or leaked out in various symptomatic behaviors. It's not really how the brain works, but it has had a certain limited functionality anyway.

During the early 1960s, our Harvard Psychedelic Drug Research project studied the reactions of thousands of subjects during psilocybin and

LSD sessions. We were able to recognize and classify the standard range of psychedelic-hallucinogenic experiences, and to distinguish them from the effects of other drugs like uppers, downers, booze, opiates, and tranquilizers. But we were able to categorize them only in terms of subjective reactions. There was simply no scientific language to communicate or model the wide range and "strange" effects of these chaotic phenomena. Psychiatrists, policemen, moralists, and people who did not use drugs accepted the notion of "psychotomimetic states." There was one normal way to see the world. Chaotic drugs caused all users to lose their grasp on the one-and-only authorized reality, thus mimicking insanity.

To talk and think about drug-induced experiences, the Harvard drug experimenters and other researchers were forced to fall back on the ancient literature of Christian mysticism and those oriental yogic disciplines that had studied visionary experiences for centuries. The scholars of mysticism and spiritual transcendence snobbishly tended to view "normal reality" as a web of socially induced illusions. They tended to define, as the philosophic-religious goal of life, the attainment of altered states.

Needless to say, enormous confusion was thus created. Most sensible, practical Americans were puzzled and irritated by this mad attempt on the part of the mystical millions to enthusiastically embrace chemical insanity and self-induced chaotics. Epistemological debates about the definition of reality soon degenerated into hysterical social extremism on the part of almost all concerned, present company included. Arguments about the nature of reality are always heavy, often bitter and emotional. Cultural, moral, political, racial, and above all, generational issues were involved in the Drug Wars of the late 20th Century.

But the basic problem was semiotic. Debate collapsed into emotional babble because there was no language or conceptual model of what happened when you got "high," "stoned," "fucked up," "loaded," "wasted," "blissed," "spaced out," "illuminated," "satorized," "god-intoxicated," etc.

Here again, external technology can provide us with an updated model and language to understand inner neuro-function. Television became popularized in the 1950s. Many psychedelic trippers of the next decades tended to react like television viewers passively watching the pictures flashing on their mind-screens. The semantic level of the acid experimenters was defined by the word "Wow!" The research groups I worked with at Harvard, Millbrook, and Berkeley fell back on a gaseous, oriental, Ganges-enlightenment terminology for which I humbly apologize.

Then, in 1976, the Apple computer was introduced. At the same time video games provided young people with a hands-on experience of moving flashy electronic, digital information around on screens. It was no accident that many of the early designers and marketers of these electronic appliances lived in the San Francisco area and tended to be intelligent adepts in the use of psychedelic drugs.

Those young, bright baby-boom Americans, who had been dialing and tuning television screens since infancy, and who had learned how to activate and turn on their brains using chaotic drugs in serious introspective experiments, were uniquely prepared to engineer the interface between the computer and the cybernetic organ known as the human brain. They could handle accelerated thought-processing, multilevel realities, instantaneous chains of digital logic much more comfortably than their less-playful, buttoned-up, conservative, MBA rivals at IBM. Much of Steve Jobs and Steven Wozniak's astounding success in developing the Apple and the Mac was explicitly motivated by their crusade against IBM, seen as the archenemy of the 1960s counterculture.

> ## But you're taking a risk every time you breathe the air; every time you eat the food the supermarkets are putting out; every time you fall in love.

By 1985 millions of young Americans had become facile in digital thought-processing using inexpensive home computers. Most of them intuitively understood that the best model for understanding and operating the mind came from the mix of the psychedelic and cybernetic cultures.

In the '70s, hundreds of New Age pop psychologists, like Werner Erhard, taught folks how to reprogram their minds, write the scripts of their lives, upgrade thought-processing. At the same time, the new theories of imprinting, i.e., sudden programming of the brain, were popularized by ethnologists and hip psychologists like Conrad Lorenz, Niko Tinbergen, and John Lilly.

Once again, externally engineered tools helped us understand inner function. If the brain is viewed as bio-hardware, and psychedelic drugs become "neurotransmitters," and if you can reprogram your mind, for better or for worse, by "turning on," then new concepts and techniques of instantaneous psychological change become possible.

Another relevant question arises: Can the computer screen create altered states? Is there a digitally induced "high"? Do we need a Digital Enforcement Agency (DEA) to teach kids to say "No," or more politely, "No, thank you" to RAM pushers?

My opinion is in the negative. But what do I know? I am currently enjoying a mild digital dependence, but it seems manageable and socially useful.

In the meantime, I follow the ancient Sufi-Pythagorean maxim regarding creative writing: "If thou write stoned, edit straight. If thou write straight, edit stoned."

FAR GONE INTERVIEW

1994

Every metaphor approximating the visionary experience is optical: illumination, revelation, insight, perspective, reflection. Right down the list. Light has always been the ultimate brain experience: Tibetans talk about the White Light of the Void. Dante's Heaven was total white . . . the Egyptian religions—*sun.* These are primitive anticipations of what we now have available. The human brain is starved for electronic stimulation; the human brain is addicted to light.

RISKY BIZNESS: DANGERS & BUMMERS

1964

If the initial experience is involuntary and the setting impersonal, a most distasteful reaction is inevitable. Government-sponsored psychiatrists have regularly given LSD to research subjects in circumstances where the tripper did not know what was going to happen and where the surroundings were bleak, clinical, public, and anxiety-provoking. Such a procedure, even in the guise of science, is nothing short of psychological rape, and it is exactly this sort of impersonal laboratory experimentation which has given LSD a bad name in medical circles.

1966

When you take LSD, you're changing the system to a small degree. Most people are delighted when this happens. But when a professional full-time worrier takes LSD, he's going to wonder if he's going crazy. If he's insane, he's going to worry about brain damage, about germs, loss of precious body fluids. Worriers, of course, want everything under control. Your worrier is going to lay his worrying machinery on LSD. A Christian will take LSD and report it in terms of the Christian vocabulary. CIA agents will look for communists.

1966

Paranoia… you can find yourself feeling that you've lived most of your life in complete isolation, not really touching and harmonizing with the flow of the people and the energies around you. It might seem to you that everyone else, and every other organism in creation, is in beatific communion, and only you are isolated by your egocentricity. Every action around you fits perfectly into this paranoid mosaic. Every glance, every look of boredom, every sound, every smile becomes a confirmation of the fact that everyone knows that you are the only one in the universe that's not swinging lovingly and gracefully with the rest of the cosmic dance. I've experienced this myself.

1967

The typical LSD bad-trip panic occurs when the subject discovered the rubber-stamp, artificial nature of social reality and social role; realized that one's identity is a fragile role in a flimsy historical vaudeville show. This freedom is wrong! Get me back to my safe cubicle in the urban hive! If I am not my social role, who am I? What will the neighbors and the moralists think? If I violate the taboos defining my cultural identity, I will offend God.

1977

If nobody knows exactly what LSD does—and I share that worry—we must realize that scientifically we are not sure of the effects of gas fumes, DDT, penicillin, tranquilizers on the individual and the genetic structure of the species. There are risks involved. Nobody should take LSD unless she knows she's going into the unknown, laying her blue chips on the line. But you're taking a risk every time you breathe the air; every time you eat the food the supermarkets are putting out; every time you fall in love. Life is a series of risks. We insist only that the person who goes into it knows it's a risk, knows what's involved. No paternalistic profession like medicine has the right to prevent us from meeting that challenge. If you listened to neurologists and psychiatrists, you'd never fall in love.

* * * * *

PART 2: ARGUMENTS

1966

The analogy I use is drawn from the science of optics. Three hundred years ago, if I had announced there was a level of reality made up of tiny particles which seem to have a beauty, a meaning, and a planning of their own, I'd be in danger of being imprisoned. When I could persuade people to look through the microscope lens at a leaf, or a snowflake, or a drop of blood, *then* they would discover that beyond the macroscopic world are visible realms of energy and meaning. But if I had clapped a microscope onto your eye 300 years ago and said, "Walk around this," you might trip over things. You might be entranced by the beauty of what you saw, but you'd end up quite confused: "Well, it's rather crazy and meaningless. I couldn't see anything I recognized."

The use of the microscope required that certain men spend hours peering through lenses at different forms of biological energy, and very slowly and painstakingly develop a language. I could write a handbook explaining the different sorts of things you could see when you looked at a cross-section of a plant. And then you could look through the microscope and check out my accuracy.

Similarly, there are levels of consciousness, defined by the anatomical structures within the brain for decoding energy. And each level of consciousness is inevitably produced by biochemical means, either by natural, biochemical events or by introduced chemicals that move you to these different levels just as accurately as the magnification of a lens moves you to different levels of external reality.

The problem is, if the unprepared person takes LSD, it's like plopping a microscope onto a man 300 years ago. Even the prepared and knowledgeable use of marijuana requires a complex yoga involving which stimuli you are going to expose yourself to; which lenses you are going to polish; which sense organs you are going to open up; a very careful arrangement of the sequence between external energy and a specific sense organ.

1966

Playboy: You don't advocate the use of LSD for simple "kicks"?
Timothy Leary: I don't know what you mean by "kicks." To me, the "kick" means an ecstatic revelation. To you, a kick may mean going to a cocktail party and flirting with some girl. A kick to me means a pagan flirtation with God—Gaia. Of course, in our Puritan society, we think we should work, get power, and use this power to control other people. In any sane society, the word "kick" could be the ideal, the ecstasy; it means going beyond, getting out of your mind, confronting God.

1968

In the fall of 1962, a minister and his wife, as part of a courageous and dedicated pursuit of illumination, took a psychedelic biochemical called dimethyltryptamine. This wondrous alkaloid (which closely approximates serotonin, the natural "lubricant" of our higher nervous system) produces an intense psychedelic effect. In twenty-five minutes (about the duration of the average sermon) you are whirled through the energy dance, the cosmic process, at the highest psychedelic speed. The twenty-five minutes are sensed as lasting for a second and for a billion-year Kalpa. After the session, the minister complained that the experience, although shattering and revelatory, was disappointing because it was "content free"—so physical, so unfamiliar, so scientific, like being beamed through microscopic panoramas, like being oscillated through cellular functions at radar acceleration. Well, what do you expect? If God were to take you on a visit through His "workshop," do you really think you'd walk or take the bus? Do you really think it would be a stroll, or a drive, through a celestial Madame Tussaud waxworks?

TURN ON, TUNE IN, DROP OUT
1968

"Turn on" means to contact the ancient energies and wisdoms that are built into your nervous system. They provide unspeakable pleasure and revelation. "Tune in" means to harness and communicate these new perspectives in a harmonious dance with the external world. "Drop out" means to detach yourself from the tribal game. Current models of social adjustment—mechanized, socialized, televised—make no sense to the new LSD generation, who see clearly that American society is becoming an air-conditioned anthill. In every generation of human history, thoughtful men have turned on and dropped out of the tribal game, and thus stimulated the larger society to lurch ahead.

FOLSOM PRISON INTERVIEWS 1973–1994

1973

Q: Even though you say that LSD is safe, do you think that you have suffered any brain damage whatsoever?

LEARY: That's a very tricky question for anyone to answer. I'm fifty-two. I think that anyone who's still erect after these last five decades has had his sanity tested. I've been through a lot of rough times. My career has been ruined. I've been in twenty-four prisons, all without committing any crime that I know of. In addition, I've probably pushed my nervous system as much as any human being alive. I've taken LSD over five hundred times and experienced a wide range of biochemical and neurological possibilities.

Is there any objective way to test your sanity? Well, people who get to know me seem to think I'm pretty sane. I've written two books in the last few months. My book *Hope Fiend* earned me a quarter of a million dollars advance, so somebody at Bantam books didn't think I was insane. If I am insane, the government should be happy to let me out and let my insanity be apparent.

There's this ominous tendency to call anybody that you don't agree with "insane." In Russia, they put their philosophers and their dissenting poets in insane asylums. Now, maybe it is insane to hope that something could be done about what's happening in Richard Nixon's America today. But otherwise, make up your own mind.

> There's this ominous tendency to call insane anybody that you don't agree with.

1975

Why struggle for external material rewards (emotional, mental, social) which are clumsy, artificial, symbolic triggers for the sensory-somatic-endocrine experience? The external reward-triggers can be suspended by ingesting a neuro-chemical. After the adult has mastered the larval survival dials, the robot addiction to the material world can be "kicked." The high body is natural. "Normal" symbolic reality is seen as larval crutch.

There are four anti-materialist neurosomatic revelations that come to the intelligent drug user—vegetative, emotional, mental and social.

> **1. Why rely on materialistic stimuli** for the feeling of vegetative well-being, when a drug can trigger off cellular satisfaction and eliminate pain?
>
> **2. Why sweat and struggle** for the material-muscular rewards which give emotional satisfaction: the Cadillac, the title, the house on the hill when a drug can activate the neural state of freedom? Einsteinian mobility replaces Newtonian pushing.
>
> **3. Why go on repeating symbol sequences** or artifact-manufacturing processes, why continue stereotype robot mental routines, when a drug can free the mind to make new connections and fresh creative solutions? Why be a machine-like assembly-line reactor, when the loose, relaxed, floating mind can bend, curve and slide symbols in the rhythms and sequences of the natural? Why work when the universe is a playful energy field?
>
> **4. And why, for the brief pleasure** of genital orgasm, commit oneself to a life of domesticated slavery when a neurosomatic drug can produce direct, naked sensation in which every touch, taste, smell, movement, sight, sound explodes in somatic rapture?

Neuroactive drugs have been used since the dawn of history by those who wish "to escape" to the internal pleasures of the sensory-somatic.

What is it that the cannabis user escapes from? The moralistic answer: from social responsibility. The neurological answer: escape from the tunnel-reality of the survival imprints.

1977

If you take LSD, you still come back speaking English and knowing how to tie your shoelaces. That's sort of the *problem*—that you do slip back into routine ways of thinking. That's why if you take LSD, you should plan to slowly change your environment, and harmonize your external commitments with internal achievements. It's very hard work to change the human psychology. That should comfort the frightened and challenge the fast-lane, quick-change optimists like myself.

1993

There have been more than fifty million years of symbiosis, growing slowly between the vegetable queendom and the mammalian kingdom. It's no accident that we have seventy or eighty receptor sites in our brain for very specific vegetables. Was there some evil devil that gave our brains these receptor sites? Religions have demonized these vegetables, because they actually do what religious rites are supposed to do: they open up new vistas or visions, which have to do with illumination, insight, revelation.

1994

When I see a bunch of teenagers sitting around smoking pot and listening to the Grateful Dead, it fills me with despair.

1994

This study that says "Tobacco kills, #1 killer" is a total lie. Guns kill. Accidents kill. AIDS kills. Tobacco is simply lopping off the last terminal, senile years. By the way, this research was done by government researchers. You would think that any intelligent person, including the editors of the L.A. *Times*, would know that any research done by government scientists, paid for by the taxpayers, is going to come out with results that will support government policy. The way the government is demonizing tobacco smokers and drug users and alcohol… it's more flagrant than in the Puritan days. I have a table that shows the behaviors or the factors that lower the lifespan. Tobacco: Five years. Alcohol: Probably five years. The statistics say that people who die prematurely are mainly poor people. That's the cold, blunt, horrible fact. They did mention something which I've known for many years: the #1 behavior that lowers the lifespan is gluttony. I would say that the average American is dangerously overweight. This is known in Europe. They laugh at Americans because they see a busload of tourists that are all fat, and they know they're Americans. Can you imagine the problems in the heart of a 250-pound middle-class women? The strain on her heart pumping blood and oxygen through a body that is swollen twice its size? The thin person, on the other hand… well, as William Burroughs would say, "You never saw a junkie with a head cold."

1994

Unless you have some way of really activating the brain, people are going to use computers—electrons—as simply as external devices for power, control and money.

Final Reflections about Drugs

1995

In the beginning was the drug.

Terence McKenna, among others, has speculated that the evolution from prehuman to human was the result of the synergy of mind-altering plants and the human mind. It seems like a good guess. Apes, foraging for food and never having heard the word "sin," would undoubtedly have found plants that alter consciousness attractive. Dr. Ron Siegal's book, *Intoxication*, revealed in the 1980s that getting high occurs throughout the animal kingdom. McKenna points out that small amounts of psilocybin improve visual acuity, which would increase success in hunting, a definite evolutionary advantage for early protohumans.

We also know that psychedelic drugs provide insights that are pragmatically useful. Computer programmers, mathematicians and scientists report having breakthrough insights on psychedelics, including Sir Francis Crick during the discovery (or understanding) of DNA. I could go on and on contemplating the evolutionary advantages that plant-drugs, including stimulants and painkillers, might have offered prehumans.

The synergetic combination of pain and dope has certainly played an important role in Western civilization, frequently cropping up in tandem with originality in thinking. In addition to Charles Darwin, who tuned in on the web of natural life while taking opiates for his pain, I think of Friedrich Nietzsche, who battled his chronic migraine headaches with so many medicines that Stefan Zweig described the philosopher's tiny room as looking like a pharmacist's shop. I also think of Gurdjieff, whose visions of evolution from mechanistic robotry to cosmic consciousness were all written while suffering pain from war wounds and dosing himself with cocaine and hashish. I think of James Joyce, whose painful eye problems, leading eventually to blindness, were treated with cocaine and who created his hilarious non-Euclidean "in risible universe" as normal vision faded and "it darkled (tinct! tinct!) all this our funnanimal world." In the repeated cycle of pain-bliss-pain-bliss some especially gifted individuals obtain neurological vistas far beyond the reflex robotry of yokel terrestrial life.

On the Action of Psychedelic Agents

One relevant aspect of the complex action of psychedelic substances such as LSD is their ability to affect the operation of the habitual intellectual "filtering mechanisms" and allow greater detail of lower-level sensory impressions to enter the areas of consciousness usually reserved for more heavily processed signals.

The pulsating, colored geometric patterns typically observed are signals arising in the early stages of the human visual system. Their common frequency, size, and shape are correlated with neural structures in the retina. In one sense, such patterns are always present in the visual machinery. Usually, our attention isn't directed toward visualizing their operation. We are attentive to more processed interpretations of their signals that involve our having classified them in habitual categories. One identifies what is seen with one's mental model of the image, without dwelling on the details of the sensory stimulus.

Research into the exact nature of the mechanisms by which psychedelics achieve their effects remains inconclusive, although the research that ended during the 1960s by the anti-drug inquisition has finally been allowed to resume in the 1990s. Scientists are looking closely at vasopressin release and the seratonergic system. In simple terms, since seratonin limits the number of signals firing across nerve cells in the brain, a reduction in seratonin would logically allow for a greater (and possibly overwhelming) flow of signals, leading to glimpses of other interpretations of reality. In any case, the ability of psychedelic drugs to perturb, and thus highlight, the hierarchical organization of the multiple subsystems and selves within a person is evident.

Through disrupting the ordinary operation of the communicating microselves, the fractal nature of consciousness is revealed to the operator as the cerebral system compensates for the presence of excessive neurotransmitter-like substances in the synapses by rerouting signals though nonhabitual pathways. You get a glimpse at the levels of operation of this system yourself that are ordinarily below the level available for inspection. Communication between the many complex layers of one's own intellectual composition is made possible.

Contrary to feeling dissatisfied with such a highly mechanistic interpretation of the psychedelic state (so frequently dramatized in mystical terms), we are awed with the view of the realities of the human apparatus that are capable of bringing such experiences into vivid focus.

* * * * *

PART 3: THE PSYCHEDELIC MOVEMENT

By 1960, the brain had replaced the genitals as the forbidden organ that must not be touched or turned on by the owner.

—*Editor*

REFLECTIONS ON THE PSYCHEDELIC MOVEMENT

1980

In 1960–61, a group of some 35 professors, instructors, and graduate students organized what later became the Harvard Psychedelic Research Project. Core members of this influential task force included Walter Houston Clark, Huston Smith, Richard Alpert, Gunther Weil, Ralph Metzner, Walter Pahnke, Aldous Huxley, Alan Watts, George Litwin, and Frank Barron. Among the part-time participants and advisors were Allen Ginsberg, William Burroughs, Arthur Koestler, Ken Kesey, Andrew Weil, Stanley Krippner, Al Hubbard, and Gerald Heard.

Vectored into the attitude of this extraordinary company were scientific enthusiasm, scholarly fervor, and experimental dedication. Statistical morale was consistently high because the numbers looked so good!

Over 400 "subjects" shared high-dosage psychedelic experiences with the researchers in an atmosphere of esthetic precision, philosophic inquiry, inner search, self-confident dignity, intellectual openness, philosophic courage, and high humor. The historical impact of this "swarm" of influential scholars has not yet been recognized by the still-timid press, popular or scientific. The "Bloomsbury biographies" [need to be written by] the next generation.

The experimental methods and attitudes used were more important than the drugs. These neurological experiments were the first wide-scale, systematic, deliberate application to human behavior of the relativistic theories of particle behavior. Our research picked up precisely where the giant founders of experimental psychology Wilhelm Wundt, Gustav Fechner, William James, and Edward Titchener left off a long generation before. Our aim, like theirs, was the precise correlation of objective-external differences with internal conscious reactions.

Forgotten in the later hysteria of the 1960s was the exquisite design of the early Harvard experiments. Rarely in the short history of psychology was such elegant, complex, socially-influential research conducted. At the same time that the CIA was furtively dosing unwitting Harvard students for purposes of control and destruction, we were operating with the books wide open. No secrets, careful record keeping, pre-post testing. Triple-blind designs, total collaboration, the intensive training of "guides." There was extensive publication of results in scientific journals, including that impressive model of scholarly innovation, the *Psychedelic Review*.

From the first issue, we were preoccupied with the classic question: Who gets to go? Who can select the brain-drug option?

Our first answer, as scientists, was simply to publish our results and let individuals, in dialogue with society, wrangle over the answer. But it was immediately clear that every pressure group wished the "control decisions" to be made by itself. Physicians insisted that only those with MDs should decide, police would soon say no one but them, and the older wished drugs kept from the younger.

Our second answer was that any and every informed, Democratic, American adult should decide who and what to put in their own body. The question: "Who should take acid?" was a repeat of the familiar, "Who should have sex with whom? Who can smoke nicotine? Use alcohol? Wear bikinis? Drive a pleasure car? Transmit radio waves?" In democracies, these personal decisions are made by individuals and cannot be ceded to officials, all too eager to meddle in individuals' affairs.

These neurological experiments were the first wide-scale, systematic, deliberate application to human behavior of the relativistic theories of particle behavior.

At Harvard, these decisions were not made quickly. Many of our advisors urged that the drugs should remain exclusive. Gerald Heard, of blessed memory, was the most outspoken elitist: "These sacraments are powerful tools for the guild of philosophers." On the other side of the debate was Allen Ginsberg, the crusader for democratization, even socialist distribution of the drugs. Ever the worrying, nagging revolutionary, Allen [Ginsberg] howled his 1950s anarchic chant: "Turn on the world!"

There was a middle position: play ball with the Hive Establishment. Stay on government or institutional payrolls (with tenure) and reassure the commissars that psychedelic drugs can somehow produce more efficient, well-adjusted, serene soviet workers. Use the drugs to advance our positions in the bureaucracy. On to HEW! On to Stockholm! Curiously, the Harvard group never seriously considered that this "mature" option that we were acting out could last for very long.

The most influential of our number were freelance gentlemen-scholars not dependent on any bureaucracy: Huxley, Alpert, Metzner, Heard, Ginsberg, Olson, Leary, and Clark. And with few exceptions, our younger graduate students made the courageous decision to work outside the academic system. Another thought-provoking fallout from the Cambridge research: almost none of the graduate students "grew up" to become conventional, tenured, academic pensioners.

As the world came to know, our 1963 decision was to drop out of academia (helped along by a mild kick) and thereby expand our experimental design from selected laboratory samples of hundreds to field studies involving millions all over the world. We human ethnologists, activist anthropologists, left the Ivy Tower to live with the domesticated primates.

From the first paper I wrote in 1946, my obsession has been to bring objectivity to inner experiences, to demystify the software of human existence. How? By relating changes in external behavior, systematically and lawfully, to changes in the brain. Why? To give the individual, the Human Singularity, power over their own internal experiences (i.e., the brain) and over their external behavior.

This required that we work the tissue frontiers, the membrane borders where the external traffics with the internal; where the outside world interfaces with the antennae of the nervous system. For example, when we gave 100 micrograms of LSD to a subject (often one of ourselves), we were observing the effects of this measurable stimulus administered in a specified external setting on the receptive nervous system. We could not "see" the changes in the brain (yet), but we could infer them during the acid trip by measuring reactions in the form of questionnaires, reports, and behavior. And, on the broader social scale, we could observe the effects on American culture of 7,000,000 people dropping acid. We observed the effect on those who tripped and those who did not, and the collision between the two swarms.

In pursuing this goal of relating external stimuli to reports about internal-neural change, we were, paradoxically enough, following the most orthodox tradition in psychology. For performing experiments that the forgotten founders of scientific psychology would have understood and applauded, we were thrown out of Harvard and subjected to the Semmelweis Treatment.

Current psychological priesthoods ignore the fact that the profession of psychology was originated by Gustav Theodor Fechner, a physicist who recognized that the key to understanding human nature was the relationship between external stimuli and the brain.

Scientific attempts to bridge the external and the internal were begun by Sir Isaac Newton, a recognized, eclectic master of the sciences of his day. When the University of London was closed for two years (1664–66) during the plague, Newton "withdrew" from the outside world and discovered the laws of gravitation, calculus, and the theory of the light spectrum. Shortly thereafter, Newton lost interest in measuring external events and turned most of his energies "towards alchemy, theology and history, particularly problems of chronology." In other words, at the peak of his scientific triumphs, Newton became a "head," a student of the inner spiritual world. Modern physicists do not dwell on this dramatic life-change in their hero.

After Newton's attempt to relate the external-material and the internal-spiritual, physics and chemistry became mechanistic. German idealism (Immanuel Kant), British mysticism (William Blake), German Romanticism (including Schopenhauer's renovation of oriental passivity) reacted with revulsion from the scientific and tended to deny the importance, relevance, or even the existence of external movements. Thus the brilliant significance of Fechner's attempts to apply the rigor of mechanistic and mathematical science to the richness of the subjective-inner-neurological.

Since my methodology is a faithful, dutiful, follow-up to the work and life of Fechner, it may be useful to summarize this philosophic giant's extraordinary career.

Gustave Theodor Fechner (1801-87) became professor of physics at Leipzig in 1834, but ill health forced him to leave in 1839. His "illness" was clearly neurological or psychosomatic. He lay in bed for a year, unable to see, communicate, or locomote. This "sensory-social deprivation" ended one day when he rose, walked to the garden, looked around, and announced that all life was a unity. The rest of his career was devoted to "scientizing" the internal ineffable. Two of his most important books were *Zend-Avesta* (1851) and *Elementen der Psychophysik* (1860). He maintained that life is manifested in all objects in the universe.

Note that the origins of scientific psychology were called psychophysics; that Fechner wrote a book on psycho-aesthetics. The importance of these concepts has been ignored by the mechanistic psychological bureaucracies that have domesticated psychology for the last 60 years. The recent history of philosophy-science is nothing less than the ancient struggle to relate body and mind, i.e., the external-mechanistic with the internal-neurological.

Brass-instrumented laboratories popped up in Germany, England, and America. Psychology was called "introspectionism." The subject used in experiments was a "trained introspectionist," i.e., one who could purify her mind of extraneous thought and concentrate on "J.N.D.'s" (Just Noticeable Differences) in external stimuli. Which weight felt heavier? What were the discriminated units of perceived taste, smell, kinesthetic sensitivity? Sensational psychology. But during the 1920s, Ivan Pavlov and John Broadus Watson glorified raw-radical mechanistic behaviorism and denied the existence of consciousness as a scientific datum. At the same time (and these polarities seem to be perfectly synchronized according to laws of cyclical development), Freud and his diverse followers focused on consciousness and unconsciousness.

Scientific attempts to bridge the external and the internal were begun by Sir Isaac Newton, a recognized, eclectic master of the sciences of his day.

Socialism, communism, and liberal-rationalism tended to stress the material. Right-wing thinkers stressed the romantic-spiritual. The caricature extremes of this polarity are illustrated by the mass murderer Adolf Hitler: a romantic vegetarian, a student of the occult, who believed in race, blood, soul, genetic-chauvinism, social Darwinism, destiny, drugs, vision. And on the other side, the mass murderer Stalin who killed perhaps 20,000,000 in the name of dialectical materialism, socialism, and economic progress, and Mao who killed at least as many for the same cause.

By 1960, both the psychoanalytic and the socialist-materialist dreams began to fade. Psychophysics boomed back with a bang—although now it is called neurophysics, more commonly known as the "head-trip." Almost everyone began popping brain-change pills to alter moods, perspectives, realities. From middle-class Valium addicts to "reward-yourself-with-a-light-beer-after-work" drinkers to potheads, over 80,000,000 Americans caught on that brain function can be changed by one simple behavior—put a specified chemical into your body.

Predictably enough, most of those who used drugs during the 1960s and

1970s glorified the drugs and raved incoherently about inner experiences, but failed to realize that the brain was the key. The very term "consciousness-expanding" (or "consciousness-altering") drug is a primitive, prescientific concept. The precise terminology is "brain-change-drug." We often preferred the term "brain-reward-drug." These verbal distinctions are not petty or pedantic; the Brain is the key. The Brain is the source. The Brain is God. Everything that humans do is Neuro-ecology.

In the fall of 1959, I taught behavioral psychology at the University of Copenhagen by day, and by night learned experiential psychology in the port-town's psychlotrons. Eighteen months later, respectably perched at Harvard, I received a letter from a friend, a professor of psychology in Denmark: Copenhagen had been selected as host city for the 1961 convention of the International Association of Psychology. My friend confided that Danish psychology was suffering from an inferiority complex in relation to medical psychiatry, and that the Psychology Department fervently hoped that the international congress would establish the credibility and respectability of psychology, thus resulting in increased federal funding.

The conference was scheduled in smorgasbord style: visiting psychologists had their choice of some twenty seminars or presentations at any time except for the first day, which was devoted to three general convocations. Could I help in suggesting keynote speakers for the three plenary sessions? Sure thing, Bjorn.

The Game Theory subtly undermines the cultural authoritarianism that forces people to play rigid parts in games that they themselves do not select.

We quickly agreed on a slam-bang opening day. The conference would open in the morning with a lecture by Harvard Professor Harry Murray: elegant, courtly, romantic, high cultural dean of personality psychology. For the afternoon plenary, my suggestion of Aldous Huxley was enthusiastically accepted. The distinguished British author was a favorite of the anglophile Danes, who knew him as a sophisticated novelist. (As it turned out, the genial Danes were unaware that Huxley's recent books were devoted to consciousness-altering drugs.)

The evening plenary session, chaired by me, focused on new methods of psychotherapy. In addition to my major lecture, there would be contributions by my brilliant, innovative friend-mentor Frank Barron, who had introduced me to the use of psychedelic drugs. Also scheduled was Richard

Alpert, my partner in the Harvard Psychedelic Drug Project.

A few weeks before the conference, Professor Murray walked into my Harvard office with the congress schedule in his hand, chuckling: "You've subverted this sedate, boring conference into a wild bohemian drug session, haven't you?" I smiled and nodded. "In that case," replied the suave Professor Murray, with a twinkle in his eye, "I guess you better guide me through one of your visionary trips. I can't be left behind by literary romantic upstarts like you and Huxley." And so it came to pass that Professor Murray came to my home and, propelled by psilocybin mushrooms, voyaged to uncharted realms of his own neurology.

Professor Murray opened the congress by announcing that after taking a psychedelic trip, he had shelved his prepared lecture in favor of a new topic: "New Visions for Psychology's Future." Not a bad beginning! In the afternoon, Aldous Huxley took the enormous gathering of solemn-faced academicians through *The Doors of Perception.* As we left the Queen's Palace Auditorium, three members of the Danish psychology faculty rushed up to me complaining bitterly and waving newspapers. One top headline read: "I WAS THE FIRST SCANDINAVIAN REPORTER TO TRY THE POISONOUS MUSHROOMS FROM HARVARD." Covering the front page was a photo, magnified to 12 gleaming inches, of Richard Alpert's eye, dilated, popping out wildly. Underneath, the photo's caption read: "I can control my insanity, says Professor Alpert of Harvard." It seemed that Richard Alpert (in later years, to become a Hindu holy man named Baba Ram Dass) had the night before been partying with some members of the press and had been persuaded to turn on a reporter.

"You are making fools of us!" shouted the Danish psychologists. "You Americans don't understand. Denmark is a very little, cozy, quiet country. Scientists are not supposed to perform experiments that are reported on the front page." I reassured them that the evening's program would be impressive and history-making. And I promised them that during the rest of the congress, Richard Alpert would not turn on any more Danes.

That evening I delivered a lecture, partially reprinted here, that subsequently was reprinted in psychology textbooks and several reference volumes. It is considered a classic, influential work because it introduces the notion that human behavior can best be understood in terms of "games." For example, the position "husband" in the Game of Marriage is seen as comparable to a position of, say, "outfielder" in the Game of Baseball. The Game Theory is a very subversive, meta-social concept. It implies that you are not just the role that you-and-society have fabricated for you. It encourages flexibility, humorous detachment from social pressures. It allows you to change "games" and positions without the shame-stigma of being unreliable or undependable. It allows people to study, and even measure, their performances, and to seek coaching. It endorses changeability and an amused-cynical liberation from "hive" pressures. The Game Theory subtly undermines the cultural authoritarianism that forces people to play rigid parts in games that they themselves do not select.

Another "historic" contribution of this essay: it presented, for the first time, the notion that in order to change behavior (external performance), it is necessary to change your inner experience, i.e., your neurology. Here you will find an archeological curiosity: the first advocacy of brain-change drugs, not as medicines to cure disease, but as self-employed instruments to improve, change, and manage one's consciousness.

After scholarly presentations by Professor Frank Barron and another respectable psychologist, Richard Alpert walked to the podium and shocked the audience—me included!—by announcing that the visionary experience was an end in itself, and that the drug-induced religious-mystical trip produced love, Christian charity, and the peace that passeth understanding. This final straw broke the back of scientific respectability. Psychiatrists leaped up and, in seven languages, denounced nonmedical psychologists discussing drugs, berating the notion of drugs used for growth instead of cures for disease. For the angry psychiatrists, there was much applause.

Later, at our hotel suite, we were joined by three Danish psychologists who looked at me with melancholy reproach. "You have set Danish psychology back twenty years."

"Not at all," I cried, filling their glasses with aquavit and their brains with positive electricity. "You have just hosted the most important congress in the history of psychology. The annals of science will record that in Copenhagen, psychology became a true science of brain change. I bet you a bottle of champagne that in twenty years this conference will be compared to those moments in history when Newton and Darwin spoke before the Royal Society." We continued abusing the dangerous Danish drug and left on good terms.

Fragments from lecture at International Association of Psychology

1961

In our research endeavors, we developed egalitarian principles to determine role, rule, ritual, goal, language, and value, and to define the real, the good, the true and the logical. Any contract between humans should be explicit about any temporary suspension of these equalities. Two research projects attempted to put these egalitarian principles into operation.

In one study we administered psilocybin, in a naturalistic supportive setting, in order to observe the rituals and language Americans impose on an intense brain-change experience quite alien to their culture. One hundred and sixty-seven subjects—43 females and 124 males—were given psilocybin. Of these, 26 were scholars, artists, medical doctors, professional intellectuals; 21 were "normal: nonprofessionals, 27 were drug addicts (psychological or physical); and 10 were inmates of a state prison. In most cases, the drug was given only once, under informal (non-laboratory) conditions, with no attempt to be therapeutic or problem oriented.

> ## Richard Alpert shocked the audience—me included!—by announcing that the visionary experience was an end in itself, that the drug-induced religious-mystical trip produced love, Christian charity, and the peace that passeth understanding.

Seventy-three percent of our subjects reported the psilocybin experience as "very pleasant" or ecstatic; 95 % thought the experience had changed their lives for the better. Three out of four reported happy reactions. The most common reaction reported was the sudden perception of the effects of abstractions, rituals, learned-game routines: ecstatic pleasure at being temporarily freed from these limitations.

You cannot sensibly talk about the effects of a psychedelic drug without specifying the set of the subject and the environmental context. If both are supportive of self-discovery and aesthetic philosophic inquiry, a life-changing experience results. If both are negative, a hellish encounter can ensue. Of course, people tend to impose familiar games onto the psilocybin experience. If the drug-giving person is supportive, flexible, and secure, then the experience is *almost guaranteed* to be pleasant and therapeutic.

Many of the 167 subjects in our study were already involved in rewarding games to which they could return with renewed vision and energy. But many of our subjects came through the psilocybin experience with the knowledge that they were involved in nonrewarding games, caught in routines they disliked. Many of them moved quickly to change their life games. For others, the "therapeutic" effect of the experience did not last. They were left with pleasant memories of their visionary journey and nothing more.

The second experiment involved 35 volunteer prisoners in a maximum-security prison. The recidivism rate is 80%. Twenty-eight would be expected back in prison within a year. In baseball terms, 80% is the error percentage our team attempted to lower.

The drug was given after three orientation meetings with the prisoners. The psilocybin session was followed by three discussions, then another drug session, then more discussions. In some hundreds of hours of mind-blown interaction, there was not one moment of serious friction or tension. Pre-post testing demonstrated dramatic decreases in hostility, cynicism, depression, and schizoid ideation; and definite increases in optimism, planfulness, flexibility, tolerance, and sociability. The psilocybin experience made these men aware that they had been involved in stereotyped "cops and robbers" games of being tough guys, of outwitting the law, of resentful cynicism. "My whole life came tumbling down, and I was sitting happily in the rubble," said one prisoner.

The group has become a workshop for planning future games. Some prisoners are being trained to take over the functions of a vocational guidance clinic. They are preparing occupational brochures for inmates about to be released, making plans to act as rehabilitation workers after their release. They are also organizing a halfway house for ex-convicts. Other prisoners are using their time to prepare for the family game, or the old job game to which they will return.

Of course, our new game of allowing criminals to take over responsibility, authority, and prestige brings us into game competition with the professional middle class. If criminals are no longer criminals, where do the rest of us stand? People are upset when their games are changed.

Those who talk about the games of life are invariably seen as frivolous anarchists tearing down the social structure. Actually, only those who see culture as a game can appreciate the exquisitely complex magnificence of what human beings have done. Those of us who play the game of "applied mysticism" respect and support good gamesmanship. You pick out your game, learn the rules, rituals, concepts; play fairly and cleanly. Anger and anxiety are irrelevant, because you see your small game in the context of the great evolutionary game which no one can lose.

Many of those to whom we gave psilocybin were financially dependent on being creative. Artistic and literary folks respond ecstatically and wisely to drug experience. They tell us that this is what they have been looking for: new, intense, direct confrontation with the world about them. Poets and painters have always tortured themselves to transcend space/time boundaries by every means possible. At certain historical time-places, when political-economic security allows breathing space from survival pressures, entire cultures invariably "get high" on brain-change techniques. In the Khajuraho culture (c.a.d. 1000), an entire society collaborated in constructing enormous temples covered with erotic carvings. The Konarak culture (c.1250), again mobilized the energies of a generation in constructing acres of sexually explicit temple sculpture. A similar thing happened during the Mogul period, 17th century, in North India, when the Taj Mahal and other esthetic-erotic constructions dominated social consciousness. The prevalence of mind-changing drugs (several Mogul emperors were notorious hashish-opium smokers) and mind-changing yogic methods undoubtedly stimulated these amazing peaks of artistic expression.

DRUGS ARE THE ORIGIN OF RELIGION AND PHILOSOPHY

1983

Robert Gordon Wasson (1898–1986), born in Montana, grew up in Newark, New Jersey. A banker by profession, Wasson climbed the corporate ladder to become vice president of J.P. Morgan & Co. Working with his wife, Valentina, Wasson also gained recognition as an ethnobotanist, specializing in the role of hallucinatory mushrooms in the history of culture.

In 1965, Wasson became the first white person in recorded history to eat "sacred mushrooms," which were administered to him by Maria Sabina, the renowned Oaxacan witch. His are probably the most poetically moving and philosophically convincing accounts of drug-induced experiences ever published. *Mushrooms, Russia and History* (1957) was the first of several books by Wasson that traced the origins of many world religions to psychedelic-mushroom or lysergic-acid cults. Wasson's research in mind-altering plants led him to Mexico, Japan, India New Guinea, and Afghanistan. He served as Honorary Research Fellow at the Botanical Museum of Harvard University and as Honorary Research Associate and Life Manager at the New York Botanical Garden (Spring, 1960).

Around the corner from our Center for Personality Research was the Harvard Botanical Museum, the lair of the world's leading ethnobotanist, Professor Richard Evans Schultes. His specialty: psychoactive plants. Professor Schultes had spent years up the Amazon during and after World War II, scouting rubber sources for the American government. To while away long nights in the field, the diligent botanist experimented with various mind-altering herbs, roots, and vines used by the natives. He reported that for eight years he chewed coca leaves on a daily basis for energy and euphoria. Considering his openly expressed, right-wing political views and continued government sponsorship of his work, few were surprised to learn (in *Acid Dreams: THE CIA and the Acid Generation* by Lee and Schlain) that his reports were used by the CIA in its brainwashing experiments during the 1950s and '60s

As novices in the visionary field of psychobotany, we in the Harvard Drug Project viewed Professor Schultes with the respect due to an intrepid scholar. It was our custom to drop by the museum to ogle the specimens displayed discreetly in glass cases. Schultes was always cordial to us, but distant. We felt like natives, whose drug habits he was observing.

One day we received a call from Schultes' office at the museum. On the line was Robert Gordon Wasson, who was made famous by a long article in *Life* magazine that described his treks to Mexico and his discovery of psychedelic mushrooms. Before Wasson, most mycologists had denied the existence of the magic mushrooms. Wasson proved them wrong. The dignified Manhattan banker had taken the mushrooms, lain down on the mud floor of an Oaxacan shaman's hut, and experienced profound philosophic visions.

Wasson made subsequent trips to Mexico with Roger Heim, a distinguished French mycologist. They sent specimens to the drug laboratories of Sandoz, where Albert Hofmann, who had discovered LSD, synthesized the active ingredient. So we owed our psilocybin supply to the diligence of a New York banker and the craft of a Basel chemist.

Wasson asked if he could come around to visit. We arranged a high-tea ceremony in the center conference room.

Banker Wasson was a good-looking guy with a serious manner.

We listened as he told us about his first psychedelic experience and the hypothesis that led him to seek it out.

"I do not recall," said Mr. Wasson, "which of us—my wife or I—first dared to put into words, back in the forties, the surmise that our remote ancestors, perhaps 4,000 years ago, worshipped a mushroom. In the fall of 1952 we learned that the 16th Century writers describing the Indian cultures of Mexico had recorded that certain mushrooms played a divine role in the religion of the natives. The so-called mushroom stones (found in Mexico) really did represent mushrooms. They were the symbol of a religion, like the cross in the Christian religion or the star of Judea or the crescent of the Moslems. Thus we find mushrooms in the center of the cult with, perhaps, the longest continuing history in the world."

Cheerful glances crisscrossed the room as we hear our psychological research being linked with an impressive historical precedent. This was the sort of pep talk we hungered for.

"The advantage of the mushroom is that it puts many, if not everyone, within reach of a visionary state without having to suffer the mortifications of Blake and St. John. It permits you to see vistas beyond the horizons of this life. To travel backwards and forwards in time. To enter other planes of existence. Even, as the Indians say, to know God.

Dick Alpert, seeing how our credit rating would rise with this Morgan Bank testimonial, told Wasson about the content analyses we were making of the writings of visionaries and philosophic drug users. He mentioned our plans to develop a scientific classification model of the levels or circuits of the nervous system and our plans for an Experiential Typewriter (subjects could press appropriate symbol-keys instead of struggling with words.)

But Wasson hadn't come to listen. He'd come to tell us about his first drug trip.

Wasson was playing gentleman pedant to the hilt, savoring his position as Honorary Associate at the Harvard Museum as only a civilian could. He delighted in the recitation of the scientific names for plants. Peyote was *Lophophora williamsii,* synonym for *Anhalonium lewinii,* named to honor Lewis Lewin. Lysergic acid turned up as *Rivea corymbosa,* the morning glory seed. Junkies were addicted to *Papaver somniferum,* and that white powder that Hollywood producers and Wall Street bankers would soon be stuffing up their noses was *Erythroxylon coca.*

It was somewhat disappointing. Wasson had safaried down his cerebellum and had come back, like most khaki-clad nineteenth-century explorers, expecting to stake the claim on these undiscovered regions. He didn't want to hear that we had ventured into this same territory. They were *his* fucking mushooms controlled from his Maker's boardroom. He seemed to view us as rivals. I made a mental note to phone Aldous Huxley about how to deal with colonial competition.

Wasson suggested that every major world religion had originated in the botanical hallucinations of some early visionary. He recited and then translated the ancient names for mushrooms in various Middle Eastern and Oriental languages, proposing that they all implied a religious experience—food of the gods, flesh of the gods. Even the name of Jesus Christ in Aramaic, he claimed, was derived from the word for psychedelic mushroom.

But Wasson was opposed to any current use of the mushrooms. Although these fungi had produced all of the great philosophic visions of antiquity, he proclaimed, they had no relevance to the modern world. During our conversations, Wasson made it clear that he was the only one capable of explaining the mushrooms, and he was proud that he published his reports in respectable journals and in magazines like *Life*. He was particularly upset that mushroom visions had been published in "vulgar" magazines. He expressed approval of police raids on "oddballs"—young people who used the psychedelic mushrooms for personal growth and spiritual discovery.

Ironically, his writings inspired numbers of young people to descend on such villages as Juatla to share the experiences he so eloquently described. Wasson's possessiveness puzzled me. He approved of raids by the *federales* on these youthful searchers, and he made no protest when Maria Sabina was arrested soon after.

Insisting that the shamans ought to remain silent about their work, he then expressed guilt that he had broken the secret circle and published its ceremonies. He said airing the cult secrets destroyed their power.

ACID GOES POP

1983

In 1966, about the time that *Newsweek* ran a cover story on marijuana as a new middle-class recreational drug, we started hearing rumors that Henry Luce had inspired his editors to do a major story on LSD. *Life* hit the stands in March, the cover shouting, "TURMOIL IN A CAPSULE— One dose of LSD is enough to set off a mental riot of vivid colors and sites —or of terror and convulsions." Four pages of pictures showed a teenage girl having a scary trip. An objectively sober article by Barry Farrell reported: "An all-fronts movement has sprung up . . . on big city campuses and in intellectual circles all over the Western world, and it comes complete with quarterlies, lecture courses, a barrage of guidebooks to the cosmos and even two or three psychedelic churches.

"There are many others whose interest in the drug has nothing to do with psychic revolution. Mathematicians have used it as a lens through which they sometimes glimpse the physical reality of concepts that the mind can only imagine—advanced number theory, for example . . . There are psychedelic corporation presidents, military officers, doctors, teachers—each with a reason to risk a voyage on the unpredictable terrain of the deep brain dreamscape."

Billy Hitchcock was photographed in front of the Big House for this article. Walter Clarke was pictured in his study, saying, "These drugs present us with a means for studying religious experiences in the laboratory. No psychologist of religion can afford to be ignorant of them." A retired Navy captain, John Busby, claimed to have "solved an illusive problem . . . developing intelligence equipment for a navy research project" while under the influence. A hardheaded Republican businessman became God while tripping.

In spite of the hand-wringing, the *Life* essay amounted to a most convincing endorsement of LSD and an eloquent plea for non-medical research. It was obvious that Henry Luce's commercial would double the number of consumers, most of whom would be unprepared. With millions of people taking the drug it was certain that occasional bad trips would start to add up.

A Sociology of LSD
1988

In 1973, the Federal Drug Agency estimated that more than seven million Americans had used LSD. When this number of young and/or influential people engages in an activity passionately denounced by every respectable organ of society as dangerous, chaotic, immoral, and illegal, we have a social phenomenon that is worthy of study. Here is a fascinating development: a new sin! A new counterculture. A new evil crime.

I hope the following observations will encourage anthropologists and sociologists to undertake more systematic analysis of the survival implications of this mass behavior. Even a Gallup poll in which users could describe the effect that LSD tripping had on their lives might produce provocative data if we are ready to face the facts.

It Was Just One Of Those Times

The postwar baby-boom generation that came into adolescence during the 1960s was probably the most affluent, confident, indulged human crop in history. Many social forces conspired to encourage this group to expect and demand more from life. The '60s kids were free from the economic fears that had dominated the lives of their depression-scarred parents. America was in a period of expansion and growth. Recruiters from large businesses used to line up on campuses to beg students to consider well-paying jobs! The nuclear fears that plagued the 1950s were quiescent. The new psychology of humanism and personal growth, developed by Carl Rogers and

Abraham Maslow; encounter groups; and other developments of the human-potential movement reactivated the basic Emersonian values of self-exploration, self-reliance, and transcendence of fear-inspired ortho-doxies. The art world, always seminal in countercultural change, seethed with the effects of expressionism, improvisation, and individualism. Even the staid physical sciences were exploding with evolutions based on theories of Einsteinian relativity, Heisenbergian alternate realities and expanding universes.

This had happened before. At similar moments in history when cultures reached similar states of national security, economic prosperity, and imperial confidence, the inevitable next step has been to look within. A counterculture encourages novel art forms and lifestyles and tolerates individual search for new meaning and self-indulgence (as opposed to survival drudgery and the coerced indulgence of elite rulers). Exactly at these times when philosophy, science, art, religion vibrate with transcendent energies, two things often happen: external exploration into undiscovered geographical realms, and inner exploration using brain-change drugs.

The first book of the *Vedás,* the West's oldest extant spiritual text, emerging at the time of the Aryan conquest of India, defined the drug soma as the basic tool for philosophic inquiry.

The Athenians were pioneer navigators: self-reliant, empirical, and dogmatic people.

The Greek mystery cult of Eleusis, which invigorated Mediterranean thought for many centuries, used an LSD-type substance (from ergot of barley) in its annual rebirth ceremonies.

The Renaissance eruption of individuality and free thought inspired great explorations, east and west, which brought back herbs, spices, and unguents that added to the hedonic movements of the time.

R. Gordon Wasson, Richard Evans Schultes, Jonathan Tot, Terence McKenna, and other ethnobotanical scholars have argued that most of the great world religions were based on inner exploration employing brain-changing vegetables. The British Empire was supported for over a century by the opium trade, which was clearly related to the flowering of romantic, mystical, transcendental thought in England. Darwin, for example, was a chronic hypochondriac and a respectable opium addict.

The acculturation of psychedelic drugs by Americans in the 1960s provides a powerful endorsement of religious rituals from the tropical latitudes. The psychedelic drugs are all derived from tropical plants. Psilocybin from mushrooms, mescaline from peyote, LSD from grain ergot, DMT and ayahuasca from tree bark and vines, and, of course, marijuana, the oldest cultivated plant on the planet. These are not the euphoriants, or energizers, or intoxicants favored by urban dwellers. Psychedelics produce states of possession, trance, delightful chaoticness, expanded consciousness, spiritual illumination, and powerful, mystical empathies with natural forces. These experiences, which are the aim of the ancient humanist, pagan religions, are the worst nightmares of the organized religions.

> **It is of sociological interest that the drug culture in America and Western Europe (and more recently in segments of Eastern Europe) dutifully re-enacted the rituals of pre-Christian pagans and polytheists.**

The so-called '60s "drug culture" was not a campus fad; it was a worldwide renaissance of the oldest religions. The hippies intuitively sensed this as they proudly wandered around barefoot, playing flutes. Paganism 101 suddenly became the most popular campus elective.

Psychiatrists, law-enforcement officials and politicians automatically assumed that psychedelic experiences were self-induced bouts of mass insanity, i.e., hallucinatory psychosis. There were no terms or paradigms in the Western intellectual tradition to explain this bizarre chaotic desire to "go out of your mind."

It is of sociological interest that the drug culture in America and Western Europe (and more recently in segments of Eastern Europe) dutifully re-enacted the rituals of pre-Christian pagans and polytheists. During the 1960s and 1970s, millions living in industrial nations used psychedelics in the context of Hindu, Buddhist, and pagan practices. Psychedelic drugs were taken in groups and in public celebrations. The acid tests. The love-ins. The communes. Most psychedelic drug users intuitively accepted the need for social bonding and tribal rituals.

The importance of group support expressed in pagan-psychedelic experiences cannot be overestimated. The psychedelic culture proudly flaunted drug taking because it was designed to produce nature loving, tribe-solidarity, humanist experiences. The first San Francisco Be-In was advertised as "A Gathering of the Tribes." This happens today at Grateful Dead concerts, when twenty thousand Deadheads routinely mingle together in dancing celebration.

Inner and Outer Space

Is it entirely accidental that our own space program, booming out to the stars, occurred exactly when our LSD-inspired inner-tripping was at its height? When the sense of national pride and confidence diminished during the Nixon years, both inner and outer exploration decreased. None of this is a surprise to any student of cultural evolution.

Can any acceptable history of our species fail to note the effects of drug countercultures and hedonic booms on the evolution of art and knowledge? Is it still too early for a scholarly examination of our current drug culture, its antecedents and consequences? Well, let's make a small beginning.

Why Did The LSD Boom Decline? We have just considered some factors that lead to the emergence of a hedonic-philosophic drug culture. Conservatives are quick to point out that transcendental, self-indulgent movements usually lead to the fall of civilizations. Didn't hot tubs, Eastern drugs, and mystical cults sap the martial vigor of Imperial Rome?

> The third generation of brain-change drugs is now appearing in plentiful quantities: designer drugs.

Probably. But we must hasten to add that it was natural and right that Rome fall. In the unbroken migration of intelligence and individual freedom from East to West, Rome had its day in the sun. But would you want to be ruled today from Italy? High civilizations do not fall; they blossom and send their seed pollens westward. Have not the descendants of the wily Sicilian Italians planted their roots today in Hollywood and Las Vegas? According to such observers as Kissinger, Herman Kahn, Reverend Falwell, and the Shah of Iran, our current hedonic drug culture represents a sophisticated corruption of the puritan American ethos. But in their self-serving zeal to restore the old morality, these imperialists fail to realize that hedonic movements go through predictable states of growth just like other social phenomena, and that the current American transcendentalism has hardly gotten started.

Hippies were the first naive, innocent, idealistic babies of the new neurological-information society. Hippies were passive consumers of the new technology, childish utopians who believed that tie-dyed clothes, Grateful Dead concerts, and parroted love slogans were the ultimate flowers of evolution.

The hippie wave declined because its members were too passive, opting for enlightenment at the nearest dealer's pad. Advertising usually does get ahead of production in the development of new culture-changing technologies, and I am ready to accept responsibility for some of that. No blame, though. When a species wants an evolutionary tool, it will get it in a generation or two. By 1970 there were, apparently, some seven million lazy consumers expecting to be given the easy ticket to brain change. Meanwhile the feds had snuffed out the few reliable manufacturers. Predictably, the land was flooded with unreliable, low-quality acid. Good-hearted amateurs collaborated with unscrupulous scoundrels to distribute an inferior product.

Thus the wholesale decline in LSD use, which stimulated exactly what the drug culture needed. Smarten up, Sister. Smarten up, Brother! People were no longer so naively utopian. They warily thought twice before tripping. And the challenge, which no sophisticated chemist could resist—to produce high-quality LSD—was thrown down.

The last two decades have just whetted humanity's eternal appetite for technologies to activate and direct one's own brain function. The drug movement has just begun.

The Third Generation of Brain-Change Drugs

The first generation of psychedelic technology involved primitive preparation of botanicals: joint-rolling, hashish hookahs, bongs. The second generation of psychedelic technologies involved the synthesis of mescaline, psilocybin, LSD, DMT, STP, MDA—all crude, Wright brothers, Model-T stuff.

The third generation of brain-change drugs is now appearing in plentiful quantities: designer drugs. Just as computers today are more efficient, cheaper, and more reliable than those of thirty years ago, so are the new drugs. Home domestication of mushrooms is one charming example.

The time-consuming, complex, delicate, unwieldy procedures for synthesizing LSD have been streamlined so that, from police reports of arrests and sociological observations, we learn that more LSD is being used today than in the 1960s. There is almost no publicity, because psychedelic drug usage is no longer a trendy topic for the media and politicians. We have new problems: oil, economics, crack cocaine, the new Cold War. There are almost no bad trips being reported, because the acid is pure and the users are sophisticated. The average suburban teenager today knows more about the varied effects of brain-change drugs than the most learned researchers twenty years ago. The proliferation of knowledge always works this way. The socialization of drugs has followed the same rhythm as the use and abuse of automobiles, airplanes, computers.

And the next decade will see the emergence of dozens of new, improved, stronger, safer psychoactive drugs. Any intelligent chemist knows this. There is an enormous market of some fifty million Americans today who would joyfully purchase a safe euphoriant, a precise psychedelic of short duration and predictable effect, an effective intelligence increaser, a harmless energizer, a secure sensual enhancer. An aphrodisiac! For millennia, intelligent persons undergoing the vicissitudes of aging have longed for an effective aphrodisiac. Only recently have we realized that the ultimate, indeed the only, pleasure organ is the brain, an enormous hundred-billion-cell hedonic system waiting to be activated.

The last two decades have just whetted humanity's eternal appetite for technologies to activate and direct one's own brain function. The drug movement has just begun.

The Resurgence of Good Old LSD

The increased usage of acid is the forerunner of what is to come, and much can be learned from its resurgence. Now that the hysteria has died down, is it not obvious that LSD—*pure* LSD—is simply the best recreational/enlightenment drug around? A curious reversal of Gresham's law seems to operate. If good dope is available, it will be preferred. If good dope is in short supply, then bad drugs will be used. Good dope drives out bad dope.

During the recent LSD shortage, did we not see a shocking emergence of teenage alcoholism? Don't you remember how drunks were scorned in the 1960s? The horrid PCP mania was directly caused by the acid drain. So were the cocaine mania, and the post-Shah heroin epidemic. Looking at the shoddy replacements, is it not clear that psychedelic drugs are exactly what our Harvard research showed them to be in the 1960s? Wonderful gifts from the plant queendom to the animal kingdom; activators of those circuits of the brain that lead to philosophic inquiry, scientific curiosity, somatic awareness, hedonic lifestyle, humourous detachment, high-altitude tolerant perceptions, chaotic erotics, ecological sensitivity, and utopian communality.

Weren't the 1960s, in retrospect, a decade of romance, splendor, optimism, idealism, individual courage, high aspirations, aesthetic innovation, spiritual wonder, exploration, and search? As President Reagan might have said, weren't we happier about each other and more optimistic when the high times were rolling?

In the Rambo 1980s, drugs were tooted, shot, free-based, and cracked in secrecy, often alone.

Drug taking becomes drug abuse when practiced in narcissistic solitude.

In 1988, thirty million Americans used illegal drugs safely, and fifty million used booze moderately. Indulgence in group rituals protects against abuse. Beer busts. Cocktail parties. Smoking grass or eating mushrooms with friends.

It is important to note that the only effective rehabilitation program for alcohol and drug abusers is A.A., started by Dick Detering, with whom I shared my first psychedelic mushroom trip. The stated aims and tactic of A.A. are pagan-spiritual. Surrender to a higher power in an intense support-group setting. No churches. No government officials. No salaries. No funding. Just village-type group support.

The Winter of our Fear and Discontent

Our psychedelic drug research projects at Harvard, and later at Millbrook, vigorously addressed the task of developing brain-change methods for eliminating human ignorance and suffering. We knew it could be done and that eventually, it *would* be done. Biochemical knowledge will be applied to manage the synaptic patterns, which keep people bogged down in repetitious helplessness. Self-managed brain control is in the future "deck."

> The only effective rehabilitation program for alcohol and drug abusers is A.A., started by Dick Detering, with whom I shared my first psychedelic mushroom trip. The stated aims and tactic of A.A. are pagan-spiritual.

This seemed so commonsensical, that, in 1962, it was hard for us to understand, how any open-minded person could oppose the planful accessing of altered states of consciousness. Granted that the field was new and the avalanche of new data confusing, the parallels to the discovery of the microscope and telescope were so obvious that we were naively unprepared for the instinctive revulsion expressed by so many intelligent, distinguished scientists at the notion of brain change. Alan Watts, always the wry student of history, never tired of reminding us that Vatican astronomers consistently refused to look through Galileo's telescopes.

Our initial romantic idealism was soon sobered by the realization that there are powerful genetic mechanisms, reinforced by society, geared to react with fear at the approach of the new. This "neophobia" obviously has a survival value. At every stage of evolution, each gene pool has been protected by those with nervous systems wired to cry, "Danger! Caution!"

The evolutionist urging change says, "There is nothing to fear except fear itself." The survivalist replies, "There is everything to fear except fear itself." At most periods of human history, those who promote fear have been in ascendance. When we examine every other form of life, we see that a nervous, jumpy animal alertness to danger is a constant preoccupation.

At certain times in the emergence of civilization, optimistic change-agents and believers in progress manage to push our species into new adventures. Then, inevitably, the forces of caution and tradition act to reimpose fear to preserve what the change-agents have created.

America has, since its conception, represented an optimistic, progressive future probe for the human race. Our country was founded by restless visionaries from the Olde World, who decided that anything new was better than the status quo. Such people are genetically wired to stir up excitement and adventure and unsettling discovery. This red-white-and-blue romantic pursuit of liberty and happiness, it seems to me, peaked in the 1960s. A generation of young Americans threw caution to the winds and recklessly rejected the fear-imposed systems that have kept human society surviving: the work ethic, male domination, racism, lifestyle conformity, inhibition of sensuality and self-indulgence, reliance on authority.

Fear, which has always been the glue that holds human hives together, was temporarily replaced by audacious, grinning confidence in a self-directed future.

Since our research had demonstrated that setting determines the course of an altered-state experience, we consistently broadcast signals of intelligent reassurance: "Trust your nervous system, go with the flow, the universe is basically a beautiful and safe place." We were amazed to witness otherwise intelligent and open-minded persons doing everything in their power to instill fear, cry danger, and slander the brain with negativity. Do we recall the hoax perpetrated by the Pennsylvania Hospital director who invented the story that eight patients were blinded by looking at the sun while high on LSD? The chromosome-breaking prevarication? The armies of police officials visiting high schools to warn that "smoking LSD" would lead to rape and murder? We were forced to conclude, at one point, that LSD does indeed cause panic and temporary insanity in bureaucrats who have never touched the stuff.

We were comforted by the history of science. Every new technology that compels change in lifestyle or understanding of human nature has always taken one generation to be socialized and domesticated. The more furious and extravagant were the attacks on LSD, the more certain we became that an important mutational process was involved.

What was lost in the furor was any rational attempt to assay what was really happening. Few Americans realized, for example, that the drug culture was the purposeful creation of an extraordinary group of scholars and people-movers who worked in loose but conscious coordination to sponsor self-directed brain change: Aldous and Laura Huxley, Gerald Heard, R. D. Laing, Alan Watts, Stanislaus Grof, Joan Halifax, Ken Kesey, Allen Ginsberg, John and Louis Aiken, Huston Smith, Cary Grant, the brigades of philosopher-musicians who used lyrics to teach, the armies of writers and underground newspaper editors, the filmmakers, the chemists. Never, perhaps since Athens and the Renaissance, had so many culturally influential people been united around a philosophic concept.

The future is going to spin faster and wilder, of that we can be sure. If you don't like acid, rest assured you're not going to like the future.

Also discarded in the controversy was any rational, scientific attempt to keep score. Granted, some mentally disturbed persons took acid and then blamed the drug for their instability, but there was never any comparative census count. Now that the smoke has cleared, we see that far from inducing window-jumping and self-destruction, the suicide rate for young people actually dropped during the LSD boom. Suicide is caused by boredom and hopelessness and certainly these factors were lowered during the 1960s.

Surely it is obvious that psychedelic drugs, including cannabis, lower the violence indices. There are more alcohol-induced episodes of violence in one weekend these days than in the twenty years of psychedelic drug taking. More kids are killed and crippled in any weekend by booze plus automobile-driving than during two decades of psychedelic consumption. There is no evidence to counter my claim that LSD drastically lowered the incidence of physical danger for those who tripped. It was Vietnam that killed more than fifty thousand young Americans and several million Vietnamese. Acid is probably the healthiest recreational pursuit ever devised by humans. Jogging, tennis, and skiing are far more dangerous. If you disagree, show me your statistics.

This is not to say that the real dangers of LSD were exaggerated. Consciousness-altering drugs change minds and loosen attachments to old customs. Change triggers intense fear reactions. Acid is a scary thing.

No one said it was going to be simple, and here is another complication:

acid should not be taken by scared persons or in a fearful setting. America is a spooked country these days. The genetic caste of danger-criers is operating in full voice. Never in our history has the national mood been so gloomy and spooky. The cause is obvious. Change causes fear, and the change rate is accelerating beyond comprehension and control. Chaotics! All the familiar comforts of yesterday are eroding with ominous rapidity. While the population rises, all the indices of intelligence, educational achievement, civility, and physical and economic security are plummeting. At the same time, paradoxically, the accomplishments of our scientific elite are eliminating the basic, eternal causes of human helplessness. Geneticists and immunologists predict enormous advances against illness, aging, and death. The space program has opened up a new frontier of unlimited energy, unlimited raw materials, unlimited room for migration. The new information society based on computers and home-communication centers is multiplying human intelligence to undreamed-of capacities. We are being flooded with new and better brain-change drugs.

The only way to understand and keep up with this acceleration of knowledge is to accelerate brain function. There are three suggested solutions to the seething, volatile situation that we now face.

> **1. The religious answer** is that since apocalypse is inevitable, the only thing to do is pray.
> **2. The politicians assure** us that the only thing to do is grab what you can and protect what you've got.
> **3. The scientific answer** is to increase intelligence, expand your consciousness, and surf the waves of chaotic change planfully.

The future is going to spin faster and wilder, of that we can be sure. If you don't like acid, rest assured you're not going to like the future. Now, more than ever before, we need to gear our brains to multiplicity, complexity, relativity, change. Those who can handle acid will be able to deal more comfortably with what is to come.

A Personal Note: People often ask me if, in hindsight, 1 would do it all over again. My answer, in foresight, is: Like it or not, we are doing it over again—and *better.*

*****

PART 4: THE TALES OF BRAVE ULYSSES

1981

I was conceived on a military reservation, West Point, New York, on the night of January 17, 1920. On the preceding day alcohol had become an illegal drug.

Academy records reveal that there was a dance that Saturday night at the Officer's Club. Now that booze was illegal, the ingestion of ethyl alcohol took on glamorous, naughty implications. The Roaring Twenties were about to begin.

My mother, Abigail, often recalled that during her pregnancy, the smell of distilling moonshine and bathtub gin hung like a rowdy smog over Officer's Row. My father, Timothy, known as Tote, was about to convert from social drinking to alcohol addiction. In training me for future life, he often told me that prohibition was bad, but not as bad as no booze at all.

At age ten, given a chemistry set for Christmas, I became Tom Swift, working to produce a drug, "Idicton," which would save humanity.

MEXICO

1963 (written 1983)

When I returned to the hotel, full of bad tidings, there was more gloomy news waiting. One of the guests, Duane Marvy, an engineer from Boston, had tripped and failed to return to normality after 12 hours. This was our first encounter with an extended "bad trip." I found him sitting on the patio, silent, unresponsive, staring at the sky. Every now and then he jumped up and tried to run away, shouting in a loud voice that we were all communists and he was going to report us to the CIA. Naturally, I thought the arrival of the police had polluted the setting. We should have suspended all sessions. I hoped that he'd snap out of it by the next day, when we all were scheduled to leave.

That night we held a final family dinner, everyone much subdued. After dessert, Dr. Fred Payne, a gray-haired psychologist who had just arrived from California, begged to have a trip. A psychiatric nurse from Menlo Park and Jack Downing, the psychiatrist, volunteered to guide him. They were so persistent that I reluctantly agreed.

An hour later, while I was sitting on the patio watching the moon, a medium-sized gorilla with the smooth skin of a naked man shuffled in, leapt on the table, beat his chest, bounded to another table, uttered a cry, and swung over the ledge into the shrubbery below.

Now began one of the silliest scenes of my life. We formed a posse of six men, armed with pillows and blankets.

A second later, Dr. Downing came running up the steps, followed by the nurse, who was out of breath. "Did you happen to see Dr. Payne come this way?" she inquired sheepishly.

"I just saw a 170-pound ape-man go through here. See if you can talk him down. And try not to play run-and-catch with him, because you are no match for a simian his size."

Swinging through the trees, dropping down on roofs, scampering up and down the stairs, Dr. Payne led his pursuers on a merry chase. When they cornered him at the kitchen door, he climbed up a drainpipe and disappeared somewhere on the upper level. The nurse and the psychiatrist came back for help.

I found Dr. Payne sitting on a stone staircase, covered with blood from superficial scratches and bruises. He was sucking his toe happily.

"Hi there, Fred. You're having a wild acid trip, aren't you?"

He stared at me in animal curiosity.

"You're going to be high for another hour or so, and then you'll start to come down. There's nothing to worry about. It's just a wild and woolly adventure you're having."

He jerked his head and sniffed the air suspiciously.

"How about a smoke, Fred?" I offered him a pack of Pall Malls. He moved towards me. Panicking, I rolled over and bumped down a few stairs. My head and my elbow were bleeding. Turning, he ran back to the upper level.

Now began one of the silliest scenes of my life. We formed a posse of six men, armed with pillows and blankets. One carried a canvas tarp and a rope. Jack Downing had a syringe loaded with a tranquilizer. We approached each cabin cautiously, flung open the door, stuck a flashlight in, and strobed the blackness inside. Then, one of us leapt in to turn on the wall switch. Cabin after cabin. None of us big-shot experts bothered to ask what exactly we were afraid of.

Finally, we saw Dr. Payne crouching on the porch in front of his own cabin. At my command, all six of us fell upon the unfortunate fellow with our pillows. He struggled a bit, but we pinned him down. Then Jack Downing stuck him with a triple dose of the tranquilizer. With the weight of our bodies, we held him down, rolled him in the tarp, wound a heavy fishnet around him for good measure, and then roped him head to toe. He looked terrible, his face bleeding, his eyes rolling wildly. As I crouched over him I happened to look up. On the roof, observing us impassively, a bottle of tequila in his hand, sat Pancho, the night security man. I felt like a foolish gringo.

We took turns sitting by Dr. Payne's side all night, but there wasn't a peep out of him.

Thinking it over, I realized that, once again, it was the people in the setting and not the tripper who had caused the problem. Dr. Payne had not touched anyone. Indeed, his every move was meant to avoid hurt rather than cause it. The only blood shed was his own, and mine when I panicked.

He was lucid, but very groggy, the next morning. Dr. Downing agreed to stay with him until they both reached San Francisco.

"We must talk about this some day," Payne mumbled to me as we bundled him off to the airport.

Duane Marvy, the spaced-out engineer, remained unresponsive. He followed me, docilely, to the VW bus taking us to the airport. We were too many for the commercial plane so the Mexican government, anxious to see us go, sent a large transport. I sat next to Marvy. He seemed to like it when I held his hand.

When we landed in Mexico City, two secret police operatives waited with a back-up squad of uniformed *federales*. It was some scene. I bought Marvy a ticket to Boston and arranged for people to taxi him home to the suburbs. When it came time to board, we tried to walk him through the gate. It didn't work. The boarding clerk took one look at the catatonic Marvy and refused to let him on the plane.

I phoned one of my Mexican psychiatrist friends who arranged to meet Marvy and me at the mental hospital in town. Checking Marvy into the hospital, I found that his wallet contained several US government cards attesting to high-level security clearances.

I sent a wire to the Defense Department: "Your agent Duane Marvy is in the Chapultepec Mental Hospital, Mexico City."

1969

After the guard completed his hostile gamesmanship, Frankie, a wise hipster in for marijuana and heroin, sidled over to me and explained the situation. "You see, that particular guard has a teenage daughter. He knows she smokes pot and lowrides with a kid who deals reds. In his mind he can see the nipples of his daughter Penny trembling under the hypnotic passes of dope pushers, her thin white legs contorted in yoga positions, offering her "flower" for the demon drug—his daughter, Penny, with fingers of limp hair bedraggled with cannabis smoke and an expression of total rapture on her innocent face. Man, he can see the pusher in his mod suit with satin cuffs propped up among the pillows on a fur-coated bed resting ermine boots on the antique coffee table, running the palm of his evil hands across the hard sharp nipples of Penny's breasts. He sees her kneeling and unzipping his pants. And you wonder why he hates you? He's not the only one. They say you don't deserve equal treatment. Can you dig that?"

Bennett, the yogi three cells over who is in for marijuana sales, begins transmitting to me the Atman Tantra, the yoga of self-love, the secret Sadhana of self-devotion. He said it was an ultimate key, a neurological technique for eroticization and maintaining a state of rapture.

He teaches me the 108 meditations of Atman Tantra. He tells me the best way to do it: "You get off on strong hashish. Then, sitting in the lotus position in a silent room, you produce an erection thinking of the most salacious fantasy that your imagination can conjure. You maintain the flowering stem while recalling one by one the 108 sexual visions."

Deprived of external stimulation, the prisoner's nervous system grows on memories. At each memory he flips a meditation bead. When he reaches the 108th he screams hreee! and explodes into a cosmic orgasm.

Deprived of external stimulation, the prisoner's nervous system grows on memories.

Bennett tells me a story. In Benares, he met a saintly old man named Yo Henbene, who had been a professor at the University but had dropped out. The old man said that all one needed in life is a crust of bread and a little hashish every day. Each morning, his disciple, Tambi, brought him a bit of hashish. He lived in a small room, totally unfurnished except for a prayer rug, a shawl, a water jug and hookah. In the next room lived a cripple with no arms or legs; a very successful beggar. One of the local prostitutes would carry him out to the street in the morning, and carry him back in the evening to feed him. Each evening the girl that he favored would put him in a basket and pick him up to fuck him, jigging him up and down. He was very virile with a big prick. As a matter of fact, that is all he was: just a head, a trunk, and a prick. The prostitutes conspired to see who would care for him. He was rich and such a weird fuck. To find a guy like that was a treasure for these girls. They had tried everything else. The old professor next door would meditate and dream and listen through the wall to the music from the beggar's room.

CIA (COUNTER-INTELLIGENCE AGENCY) REPORT ON EVOLUTIONARY AGENT LEARY IN SWITZERLAND

1972 (written 1979)

There has arrived, at Michel's chalet, a London model named Pamela whom we suspect to be an Evolutionary Agent. Please confirm. Her description is as follows: a languorous, soporiferous nervous system transported in a slender, curved body with unbearably smooth-silk arms and skin of warm sepia enamel. Her carnelian, in the form of a snail, is surrounded by translucent red enamel pierced by a Mandrax thumb.

Before dinner, while Michel is preoccupied instructing the chef, Pamela is overheard whispering to the Professor that Prince Alexis is in town. Prince Alexis—an emissary from the Rolling Stones' exile encampment in Montreux—is in town and wishes to arrange a meeting. He is to phone the chalet that evening. But Michel, deciding that a meeting between Alexis and Leary could result in an end to Leary's financial dependence, shuts off the phone.

So, just around midnight, Pamela suggests, just like a bad girl should, that Alexis might be found at the Palace Hotel nightclub, sitting, surrounded by friends, wearing an embroidered green silk shirt. Roman designers dress him *gratis*, confides the model.

The two aliens immediately recognized each other.

"Welcome fellow Time-Traveller," says the Prince. "I have come many *parsecs* to meet you."

Prince Alexis is slim and tall, with long black hair and translucent ivory skin. He looks, if it dare be said, like a fairytale prince, holding himself with royal pride, tossing his mane in fiery, petulant arrogance. Scion of a most noble family, he has been educated everywhere and done everything by age twenty-six. Gossip has it that he is sexually bilingual. He speaks Shakespearean English.

"It's taken us many orbits to get here," agrees the Philosopher. "Where was your last land-fall?"

"Katmandu. Do you know Sri Ram Muni? No? Excellent. How important that I can tell you! He knows you and has sent you a message."

"That's nice."

"I perceive," says Alexis, "a note of reserve in your voice. I share your hesitancy about Hindu swamis. I spent many months on assignment in India observing the Holy-man-groupie scene. Perhaps I should explain to our lovely companions that most of the famous swamis are hip, show-biz operators, campy-vampy-splashy-flashy queens with gullible followers, grand ashrams, and triumphal road tours, performing restful magic. It's amusing to hear them gossip and put each other down. They follow each other's productions like jealous rock stars, competing for the top of the cosmic charts."

"There are a very few Intelligence Agents left in India," agrees the Professor, "and they are as hard to find there as here. It's the classic paradox. The more advanced the mind, the fewer people to talk to."

"According to legend," continues Alexis, "there are sixty-four illuminated people in the world. You won't find them administering large bureaucracies. The real spiritual wizards in India don't solicit followings, don't open branch offices throughout the world, and can't be bothered with fans, groupies, or bank accounts."

"What do they do?" asks Pamela, leaning her head on her shoulder and moving her silken hand up her smooth arms. "Do they dance, ski, have girlfriends, get high? Are they good lovers?"

"It is my understanding," says the Professor, "that at least half of them are women. It is logical, isn't it, that many of them would be mated to each other?"

"You are thinking of Lama Govinda," says the Prince.

"And his beautiful wife Li Gotama. There's an answer to your question," says the Philosopher, turning to the Model.

"Smashing! The Holy Man and his Holy Woman," murmurs Pamela. "How original. What do they do?"

"They live in Almora," explains the Prince. "A small village in the foothills of the Himalayas. To reach Almora, one begins with a dusty train trip north of Delhi across flat, parched, semi-desert to Barelli and Katghodam. Then a bus circles up foothills, skirting gorges, crawling through dusty little hamlets where thin, barefoot men in ragged clothes run alongside, holding out empty hands, through Nainital perched like a Swiss village by the lake and up through sad, lonely, patchy, over-lumbered forests, filled with melancholic Indian army troops in dark green uniforms and pencil mustaches maneuvering to exorcize the Chinese. And finally, the bus strains up to the Holy Village on the ridge, Almora.

"This is no tourist spot, you realize, way up here, two to three days travel by semi-primitive transportation from Delhi. There is not one hotel bed in Almora. The dark rooms at the inn offer a wooden frame bed with woven rope on which you throw your sleeping bag, which, if forewarned, you have ordered, custom-made with feathers and hand-sewn cotton in the teeming market of Old Delhi. There is not one concession to European culture in Almora: not one Coca-Cola; not one modern restaurant.

> ## The real spiritual wizards in India don't solicit followings, don't open branch offices throughout the world, and can't be bothered with fans, groupies, or bank accounts.

"Now if you leave this outpost and climb a dirt road for two miles, past outlying villages, you come to Holyman Ridge, a high, steep wall which looks north across valleys to Himalayan Tibet, which towers above valleys to the south through which river and road to Katghodam curve downward. Scattered along two miles of the ridge, looking south, are houses in which assorted spiritual searchers, European and Indian, maintain part-time residence. The footpath then curves across the ridge and runs along the northern rim. This walkway, perhaps ten thousand years old, continues north to Tibet, and has been used by pilgrims, porters, merchants and, from time to time, warring bands. In a shack at the ridge-crossing, tea has been brewed for centuries in brass pots over charcoal, served heavily sweetened in thick brass mugs.

"A mile beyond the tea shack, the pilgrim leaves the main path, turns left, climbs a twisting narrow trail leading to a point at ridge-end which commands an astronaut view; north, west, and south for hundreds of miles. There, in a house built long ago by Evans-Wentz, lives the Lama Govinda and his wife Li Gotama.

"The Lama can accurately be described as venerable. An old man dressed in Tibetan robes, with a wispy Oriental beard, he is a Buddhist scholar of German descent, with an enquiring, empirical mind. Teacher, translator, transformer, transcriber, transmitter of that ancient lore, passed on by a scientific elite who devote years to research. The priests and swamis are second-hand karma dealers, who solace the masses with soothing rituals and pop-versions of hive ethical codes. But with Lama Govinda, one talks about the laws of energy that run the universe."

Alexis has been speaking intently, not paying total attention to Pamela's Mayfair pink, enamel hand on his cock or the French girl's hedonic ivory hand stroking his neck. Turning back to the Professor, he appeals for confirmation. "Isn't that what you learned in Almora?"

"Yes," says the Doctor, nodding, "Lama Govinda taught me to study the old symbol systems and to look for errors. When you find the errors and correct them, then you understand the message."

"What about Becky Thatcher?" murmurs Pamela softly.

"Ah yes," continues Alexis, "the beautiful Li Gotama, Parsee by birth, performs translations, and illustrates the Lama's books with graceful drawings. She adds the aesthetic half. Li means firelight. She calls him Ch'ien, the Creative of Heaven. I fabricate that Lama and Li are two of the sixty-four illuminated people. Would you concur?"

The Philosopher smiles in agreement.

"The Lama and Li are your teachers," says Alexis. "But I must tell you about Sri Ram Muni. He is to be found in a small temple outside Katmandu. He has preserved certain energy manuscripts that he has decoded and wishes to pass on. He has sent me West to present the version ready for you."

The Philosopher writes seven digits on a piece of paper.

"These are magic numbers," he says tipsily. "Dialed into the appropriate electronic transceptor they will put you in touch with my headquarters near Lucerne. Call me and we'll continue our talk."

[END OF TAPE]

Our local agents report that the Professor's hideout cottage on the lake has a fireplace study on the first floor, opening onto the water. The top floor is a ship-cabin sailing down the lake. From the deck, one whistles for the seven swans that float majestically along the shore and bend strong phallic necks to swallow breadcrumbs.

Prince Alexis drives up in his Stingray, dismounts regally, throws the reins to the groom and sets off a three-day cycle of life-death magic. Sitting in front of the fire, laying out some sparkly, rock star quality snow on the table, he begins to babble.

[THE CONVERSATION IS TAPED]

"The fascinating facet of India," says Alexis, "is her worship of holy putrefaction. To the banal perceptions of the West, she exists and has always existed, a bedraggled woolly mammoth, buried in the ice of occult tradition. And yet no other ancient culture has been so expressive. In stone carving, temple, wood, gesture, fluid motion, sonorous sound, she has broadcast her buoyant message to the world. Close your eyes and sleep! Lest her repetitious dream be disturbed, she asks for only the smallest dash of creative stimulus in return. Dare we introduce Western science-magic to the Ganges? Does soul, expressed in art, as in fucking, require equal reciprocity? Shall we, whether they like it or not, electrify the Sita? A rock festival in Benares?"

"Strong cocaine," says the Professor. "Can we change the dial? Let's focus on the nearby future. What part do you want to play in our next episode?"

"What is the script?"

"That is the question. We're looking for it. The womb planet waits for our next broadcast. Unhappily, it appears that we have to fabricate the treatment. What do you suggest?"

"My own obsessions are simple," replied the Prince. "Electronic rock 'n' roll along the thin aristocratic line from Chuck Berry to the Stones. Erotic mysticism, tantra and the pursuit of that Holiest of Grails: the all-night orgasmless fuck. Oh yes, my family history amuses me. The saga of decadence, Sybaritism, Epicureanism, philosophic gratification. I am, in addition, a nervous wreck. Do you know what that means?"

"I think so," replies the Professor with a tender smile.

"Then tell me quickly. Why?"

"Why what?"

"Why, when I talk to a psychiatrist does he straight-away want to pop me in treatment? It's really quite unsettling. Say something, anything, to exorcize this psychiatric curse."

"I'll have to make up a story."

"It's all fiction," says Alexis.

"In the 1960s," says the Professor, "I devoted nine years to the study of the personality, behavior, and strange beliefs of psychiatrists. They are a bizarre and superstitious tribe. My conclusion is that the profession of psychiatry is quite out of touch with reality. Do you like that?"

"Precisely my judgment," exclaims Alexis joyfully. "But I need more to convince me."

"This diagnosis does not apply to the younger generation of psychiatrists, many of whom are nice, if dull, hive agents. Freud is considered by many to be a flaming revolutionary of free and honest sexuality. Nothing could be farther from the truth. Freud was the Nixon of Psychology."

"Oh that's priceless," grinned Alexis. "Freud is the Nixon of Psychology! How?"

"Every sensible person in the world," continued the Professor, "had been trying to end the cold war, but such attempts were futile because it required someone who fanatically believed in the polarity, someone totally committed to good, to establish détente with bad. Nixon, being the last politician in the world to want peace with his enemies, had to be the one to use détente against his domestic rivals. The same thing had to happen to allow a détente between Morality and Sex in the European character structure. For, a century before Freud, every intellectual in Europe had known about the unconscious role of sexuality. But no psychiatrist or scientist with a normal, healthy sex life could be officially considered credible. It required the most uptight, sexless, prudish man in Europe to use sex as an ally against his real enemies, the Viennese medical establishment. Is that enough?"

Living ghosts disturb because they remind people that the mysteries are still alive.

"I'm a difficult case. Can you continue?"

"Psychiatry," continues the Professor, "is primitive, prescientific hive regulation. Actually, the pre-Freudian psychiatric language was much more realistic. Before Freud, psychiatrists were called 'alienists.' This is an extraordinarily happy term, because most psychiatric patients are aliens— that is to say, they have activated post-hive circuits of their nervous systems, circuits designed for future survival. When we become a space species, or if UFOs land, 'alienation' will become a very respectable word. The insane seem to live in another world. Exactly. They are, perhaps, best seen as premature evolutes. Mental hospitals *should* be called asylums. A nervous wreck is exactly that."

"It's a beautiful concept," says Alexis. "A badge of honor I shall wear proudly."

"Nervous," explains the Exorcist, "refers our attention to the nervous system, not to imaginary character traits. And 'wrecked' means 'pushed out of normal hive alignment.' Collapse of the Domesticated Mind is considered to be the goal of most mutating post-hive entities. The mind, as you know, Alexis, is the fragment of the brain that mediates the movements of the nine muscles of the larynx and the hand. Collapse of the mind means that the laryngeal muscles can no longer define hive reality."

Alexis gracefully rose to his feet and began to pace the floor. The flickering light from the fire painted red shadow patches on his aquiline face.

"Okay," he said, "that's enough for the psychiatric spell. Now, let me present you with the more serious neurological problem. I have come eight thousand kilometers to beg of you a boon. And in return I bring you a most valuable gift."

"I am at your service," said the Philosopher.

"I have fallen under a most agonizing curse."

"How was this neurological imprint imposed?"

"In India. I picked up your trail, first in the ghats and ganja shops of Calcutta. Then up to Benares, and then to Almora. It's your fault really. Your visit there has become a cultist legend. That's why I went there. In your footsteps, I found a house on swami ridge."

"Not the little cottage on Snow View which looks north to the Himalayas where I stayed with the beautiful Nordic sorceress?"

"No, nearby. But I know that cottage. I stayed in a house up beyond Snow View just before the footpath crosses the ridge."

"Just before the tea hut?"

"Yes. There are still many self-appointed holy men living along the ridge. Everyone who passes along the summit on the way to Lama Govinda's passes Snow View and feels your presence. Living ghosts make people nervous."

"Nervous is good," replied the Professor. "Nerve means courage and vitality."

It's a scandal that you are still running around this planet upsetting hive traditions.

"Living ghosts disturb because they remind people that the mysteries are still alive. It's a scandal that you are still running around this planet upsetting hive traditions. If you were transmigrated according to custom, it would be more comfortable for everyone. You could be dealt with, commercialized, marketed, rediscovered and fed into the Biography Machine. One wave of books could prove you a comic prophet. The next wave could demonstrate you were a shallow romantic, vulgarizing the ancient gnosis. In the old linear age, you would have been removed as soon as you produced a shock. If you announce you are going to drive people out of their minds, and if you do activate them to ecstasy and terror and awe, it's the genetic duty of the Hive People to assassinate you. I find your living presence disturbing. Why do you hang around?"

"Come now Alexis," murmured the Philosopher. "You are getting carried away with old pre-Einsteinian myths. Since 1946 the Genetic Intelligence assignments have changed. Agents must now illustrate, publicly and flamboyantly, the process of rapid, continuous metamorphosis. Change Agents continually change. Have some more wine."

[END OF TAPE]

"Almora," says Alexis intensely, "still trembles with the resonance-remains of vanished outcasts—magicians, as they used to call them. Did you ever freak out there?"

"Of course," laughs the Professor, "I had several splendid cosmic frights. No wonder: Siva temples, Methodist Missionaries, weird sexual cults, the underlying Hindu-Moslem antagonism, and the ominous presence of Mao across the snow peaks. If you are erotically fused, Almora is one of the highest places in the world. Were you alone there?"

"Yes," sighs the Prince. "Totally, abysmally alone."

"Tant pis. Très dangereux," exclaims the Philosopher. "If you are alone, a restless, guru-seeking pilgrim, or some such disconnected nonsense, Almora is a bore. People like Almora because it is a respectable bore."

Alexis springs to his feet shouting in pleasure. He strides across the room, leaning against the wall, begins an excited speech.

I see, in microscopic despair, these robots, who have never felt the wild Dakota wind in their face, or the taste, touch, smell, and thunder-sound of the living, eternal God.

"Exactly. It's a small bore, low caliber, dull, spiritual, Eastern colony. That's how my trouble started. One night, I found myself in the house of a group of people, many of whom you know: former students, former satellites, ex-traveling companions, an old lover, beautiful but subdued.

"Well, I hate followers, disciples, imitators. I spin out through empty space hungering for stars of equal magnitude. All right, let's face it. These middle-class people sitting around playing instruments that they can't play offended my snobbishness. I'm not that good, but I have sat in with the best groups in England and, let me speak frankly, I do own the best sound equipment in Europe. So here are these safe-and-sound people on scholarships talking Vedanta. I detest the ashram scene. YWCA tasteless. Someone starts passing acid around. I take some. Then, in disdain and irritation, I seized the box and dropped around ten pills."

"How reckless," says the Professor in alarm. "Scornful solitude is not the best space platform from which to launch an all-out voyage into time."

"Precisely. Imagine my dilemma. Almora is a spiritual Disneyland. I am now a mindless organism, a twenty-billion-neuron network flashing a hundred million signals a second— moving at the speed of light. Naturally, I tear off my artificial body covering."

Dig it, for three hours I run naked around Holy-Man Ridge in Almora, bursting with energy, shivering in cosmic loneliness, searching for a living soul.

"Naturally," agrees the Doctor.

"My brain can send messages to any of the busy little chemistry factories in my body. Pump-pump, I squirt adrenaline and ATP into my muscles. My strength has increased one hundred percent. My naked eyes see the lattice-fabric of reality. The energy is so great I literally glow. Everything is alive with electron-magnetism. And most horribly, I am surrounded by these living cores of life, encapsulated in leathery robot bodies, regarding me with distaste and fear. I am their worst nightmare come true. I am totally freaked out."

"Fantastic," smiled the Philosopher. "Priceless."

"Yes, exactly: timeless and priceless. My brain tunes into my DNA code, synapses crackling with genetic messages. I see with the eyes of countless ancestors. What a rowdy band of velvet brigands I spring from! And the *futique* children to come. You understand my predicament? I am a real entity from time suddenly trapped in this fake-believe Disneyland. Yes, that's it. I remember seeing at Disneyland a plastic Indian village with fatigued redskins selling tickets and bakelite bows and arrows to cellulose tourists. Okay, now I'm the real Crazy Horse suddenly popped down there. Whew! *Quel horreur*. I see, at a glance, what has happened to my land and my people. I see, in microscopic despair, these robots, who have never felt the wild Dakota wind in their face, or the taste, touch, smell, and thunder-sound of the living, eternal God. I scream at them, 'Are none of you alive?' I rave around looking for another living soul."

"Yes, that does tend to happen," comments the Professor, sympathetically.

"Or I am your Thomas Jefferson appearing in a modern Congress. Awake, you pink-faced, rubber frogs! Is this what we fought for! I am Giordano Bruno running around, alive in Madame Tussand's waxworks! I am Peter, the wild-eyed fisherman, screaming at the Jesus statues in the plaster Bibleland in Florida. 'Awake, brothers, let's trash this place and get back to the living soil.'

"Dig it, for three hours I run naked around Holy-Man Ridge in Almora, bursting with energy, shivering in cosmic loneliness, searching for a living soul. I sit in the lotus position on a rock overlooking the valley to Tibet and watch the sunrise. Good. That's all in order. I stalk, regally, back to the cottages, looking deeply into people's eyes. The American theosophists turn away in fear. Another acid flip-out! But dig it, the Hindu natives grin and salute me. Whew! Give me some more wine."

Prince Alexis throws himself on his knees in front of the fire and holds up his glass. The wine splashes light yellow, reflecting the firelight.

"Now, I'm getting to the hard part."

The Listener nods in understanding.

Okay, let's assume that freak-outs are created by unsympathetic, frightened people around the victim.

"Okay, I'm loping along the road, approaching the house owned by the Methodist church. Two middle-aged matron-missionaries from Kansas are standing on the steps. I love these little ladies. They were the holiest Americans I'd found in India. So I trot up to them in joyful anticipation. But dig it, they both throw up their hands in some sort of defense against me. Why? Cause I'm naked, I suppose.

"But I'm so pure. So, as I run by, I casually swing my arms and gently, the way you'd pat a push-me, pop-up doll in the toy store, knock each of them down.

"The Americans have seen me tumble the old ladies. They huddle together for a nervous conference. I can read their minds. They're afraid my antics will jeopardize their comfortable tourist scene. If only one of them had the courage and wisdom to groove with my energy, laugh acknowledgement, and run down to the river to bathe with me."

"That sounds like the sensible thing to do," agrees the Receiver.

"Now," continues the Prince, "the leader of the American colony was a solemn young professor of Sanskrit philosophy from Michigan State. He told me that he had been a student of yours, a humorless follower, who saw you as Buddha, threw himself at your feet in worship. To your dismay, I'm sure. He and his wife were visiting India on sabbatical with their two children. He notified the police."

"Oh that's too bad. Why did he do that?"

"So the policeman from the village finds me meditating at the Siva Temple. Do you remember it? It's like the Siva shrine in any village with a three-foot, stone-carved lingam that women cover with milk and flowers. The policeman waves to me and I come along cheerfully. He pops me in a shack in the village below the ridge and waits on guard for the Captain to come in his jeep. A large crowd of villagers and Americans gather around the prison shack. The Captain enters alone to talk to me.

"After twenty minutes, the Captain emerges from the shack and makes a stern, no-nonsense speech to the crowd. He says that I am a God-intoxicated saint. He tells the villagers, in Hindi, to protect me. Then he turns to the Americans. He denounces them for not taking care of their *saddhus*; for lacking faith in God's wisdom, for neglecting their holiest men. He speaks about the corrupting materialism of American culture and wonders why Americans bring their small-town concepts to spiritual India. He says that if they couldn't handle their saints, he would arrest, not the saints, but all of them."

[END OF TAPE]

The Prince and the Fugitive Philosopher are sitting in front of the fire, dented a bit by herb and wine. The sun is setting on the lake. Alexis had told his tale shyly.

"Is this the first time you've told this story?"

Alexis nods. "Yes. It's my shameful freak-out. My terrible disgrace. The Americans in Almora considered me a psychic untouchable. I've come halfway around the world to bare my neural wound."

"Do you want me to fabricate a helpful explanation of freak-outs?"

"Of course. That's why I told you my story," says Alexis, somewhat impatiently.

"Okay, let's assume that freak-outs are created by unsympathetic, frightened people around the victim. First, the nervous system retracts its imprints to hive reality and activates future circuits. Drugs can do this or it can happen naturally. When this happens, you are hyper-vulnerable to signals sent by others. You don't have your laryngeal mind to grasp reality. It hits you direct. It's a nice, free state but you are very suggestible. Now put yourself back in that situation. You are loping up to the ladies. If they had waved to you what would you have done?"

Alexis wrinkles his brow in thought. "Why, I would have waved back and trotted on. That's what happened with the Hindus."

"Good. Now, if they had fallen on their knees and prayed to you, what would you have done?"

"That's easy. I would have blessed them."

"And if they had bent over and said, 'Kick me,' what would you have done?"

'Yeah, I get the message."

"What signal did they send you?"

"They crunched up in fear as though I was a dangerous maniac."

"So, being in a cooperative mood, you gently obliged. Everything you did was perfect particle behavior. But tell me one thing. What did you say to the Captain when he came into the shack?"

"Oh, that was easy," laughs the Prince. "As soon as he entered, I murmured Om Shiva, threw myself at his feet and touched his boot with reverence. He was enormously pleased. Then we sat and he lectured me about God and Man and Law and Unity and Ramakrishna and Reincarnation. Standard Hindu Sunday School stuff. Every Indian policeman has a yen to be a swami."

[END OF TAPE]

At this point, Maria comes down with word that dinner is ready. She has prepared trout in a white wine sauce and stands by the kitchen door, Ava Gardner circa 1950, watching the cowboys in the saloon. She is a bit drunk. The Philosopher, the Prince, and the slim, hip gambler Brian Barritt escort her to the head of the table. She eats little, keeps drinking wine, then says she wants to rest. She retires to the fireplace room. She has been assigned the job of breaking up the acid scene, but the presence of Alexis, the uncertainty of her role in the new script, and the English dialogue without subtitles, overloads her circuits.

A half-hour of careful footwork and jumping leads to a narrow ledge which drops twenty feet to a sheer ice slope which ends in a hundred-foot drop.

After dinner, she sends word that she wants to see the Professor. She is lying on cushions near the fire, gasping for breath, just able to whisper that she needs medicine from her bag. Brian and the Professor search the house diligently. The bottle is missing.

Maria seems to be getting weaker. The Professor phones a medical friend in Basel who has no specific advice to give. Maria refuses to have a doctor called or to go to the hospital—shaking her classic head and rolling her dark eyes, implying that she understands the cause of the malaise. She looks into the Philosopher's eyes and whispers solemnly, *"Je vais mourir."*

The men look at each other helplessly and shrug.

Everyone in the room senses her spirit leave her body. Alexis feels her pulse. It has stopped.

Maria lays back and dies. The Professor kneels at her right and Alexis on her left. Brian Barritt's eyes are bulging. Everyone in the room senses her spirit leave her body. Alexis feels her pulse. It has stopped.

From the control tower, the Philosopher talks to her somewhere in sky-time calling her to come back. Alexis massages her heart. Like a plane circling for landing, her spirit touches down in her body and everyone breathes in relief.

"This time-travel is demanding," sighs Alexis. "Deathbed scenes are so Victorian. That's why we couldn't allow it."

Maria is now lying in the Doctor's arms, her black hair on his chest, her eyes closed, drifting in contented repose.

"What do you mean?" asks Brian.

"The deathbed scene was the climax of the classic Victorian drama. There the truth emerged. The achievements of medical science have changed all that today. We aren't interested in listening to last words. We are concerned only that the patient live. So Maria, we apologize. We brutes would not allow you to die a heroine. We treated you, alas, like a patient."

"It seemed more like a problem in astronautics to me," says Brian thoughtfully. "Who is this Maria anyway?"

[END OF TAPE]

We have attached another agent to the case, as Maria is no longer effective. His report follows:

The next day Maria seems totally recovered but refuses to discuss the matter.

After breakfast they decide to take the cable car up the Rigi

Kulm and lunch on the summit terrace. From the peak, one looks south to the four petals of Lake Lucerne and can visualize the Great Moments of Swiss history enacted below. Standing on the north parapet, one looks down to the right at Lake Zug and to the left at a long green field. It appears so close that the Prince, the Slim, Hip Gambler and the Fugitive Doctor decide to descend the cliff to the meadow and then down through the woods to the cottage. The cliff drops down in steep sections. A half-hour of careful footwork and jumping leads to a narrow ledge which drops twenty feet to a sheer ice slope which ends in a hundred-foot drop. A slip chutes the careless climber to slippery death. They start chopping footholds in the soft crumbling ice with sticks.

The climbers are wearing slick-soled track shoes; Brian and the Doctor in light sweaters, Alexis wrapped in a pink tweed coat that was given to him by Brian Jones. It is an hour before sunset. The voyagers look at each other appraisingly. Any accident will leave them exposed all night on the mountain in the February chill. They could clamber back in retreat, but without a word spoken they decide to risk going ahead together.

It takes twenty minutes of exploration and discussion to chart the descent of the first cliff. Survival circuits are flashing alarm. The sugary foothold could crumble. A foot could slip on slushy grass-mud and body slide over precipice.

The Doctor is scared; that is, the crisis centers of his nervous system energize neurons that control emergency glandular function. Each neuron has dozens of output fibers, each of which curls around a tiny bulb containing a chemical. When the alarm button sounds, fibers squeeze and danger drugs pour into the blood and lymph systems, carrying the ominous message: Attention all units, our galaxy is in mortal danger. All-out alert. This biochemical state is felt to be most unpleasant.

Alexis, at one point sliding fifty feet on the ice and bouncing to his feet without so much as a crease in Brian Jones' coat.

Alexis, being tallest and, at the moment, calmest, takes over. He digs his way down the crevice and reaches the bottom. Brian, small, wiry, cheerful, uses his foothold and quickly reaches a point where he can stand on Alexis' shoulders and then drop to the level. Much against the instructions of his warning systems, the Professor follows shakily. Halfway down, he feels Alexis's hand grab his ankle and move foot to shoulder. When he hits safety, the circuit orgasm explodes. A trillion cells receive the message: Danger alert is called off; continue normal life maintenance. The great galactic network had been mobilized for all-out survival, tested to the limit.

"The spasmodic discharge of emergency juices," says the Wizard sitting in the snow catching his breath, "is the most basic of the 24 orgasms available to the human nervous system. The roller-coaster kick."

You are, thus, being forced, one might say, by thousands of gene-pools to relive Crowley, Dr. Dee and Paracelsus.

The three climbers stand around in the late afternoon sun, smiling at each other in pleasure, like astronauts on the Ticonderoga, making speeches about how proud they are to be members of the Space program, sharing post-orgasm tenderness. They start merrily down the easy grade to the right and, within a hundred feet, make a jolting discovery. They are trapped by another steeper cliff and this time there is no easy retreat. The sun is sinking. The neural-endocrine network begins to alert for another emergency.

This time Brian leads the way, a daring slice down a small crevice, reaching his hand back to steady his companions *en route* to another adventurous, risky, daredevil, survival circuit orgasm, moving down the snow field to the next challenge. But the greatest dangers are still to come. Brian and Alexis explore the straight-ahead situation, seeking a path down the iceberg.

The Fugitive moves a hundred yards to the left where a stream plunges downward. Snow had collected in the streambed and it is impossible to progress. Working slowly, chopping ice, hanging on tree limbs, he finds a way down and shouts back to the others. It is hard for them to find him, hanging to the side of a narrow shelf, propped against a tree trunk. Now it is his turn to lead and they follow, Alexis, at one point sliding fifty feet on the ice and bouncing to his feet without so much as a crease in Brian Jones' coat.

The snow melts into a steep forest, where they hang onto tree trunks and slide down muddy paths. After an hour in the forest, they hit the high meadow, and Alexis leads them running across the ridge exultant.

Night has fallen when they reach the hotel at the base camp. The tavern-bar is civilization after a long Arctic safari. The owner finds it hard to believe that they have descended the dangerous west cliff of the Rigi in winter. They phone home. Maria has been worried. Waiting for the pickup car they order beers and lift glasses in celebratory toast.

Weeks later, Brian disclosed that it had just been another Aleister Crowley tape replay. In London, North Africa, Europe, India, Egypt, the Philosopher, guided by Barritt, has unknowingly retraced the trail of Crowley.

"It's time you realize that you are the recipient of the brain-model which is robot-wired to play the difficult public role of Evolutionary Change Agent. You are, thus, being forced, one might say, by thousands of gene-pools to relive Crowley, Dr. Dee and Paracelsus," Barritt tells the Fugitive.

"It's the Giordano Bruno script that worries me," replies the Professor.

Everyone in the lakeside cabin is now aware of the voltage released by the introduction of Prince Alexis into the molecule. Two days in a row the Death Card flashed out of the deck.

The third night, in honor of the Prince, and by way of exorcism, they arranged an alchemical experiment which involved the dissolution of hive imprints, the transmutation of realities, the reception of vibrations from post-terrestrial consciousness – 300 micrograms of LSD.

They found themselves in front of the fireplace; the familiar room now so electrified that solid objects were seen to be composed of atomic and molecular bubble-chains and lattices emitting energy. A low comfortable humming sound filled the air.

After innumerable re-imprinting exercises, Alexis smiled and produced from his briefcase the ancient leather text, which had been sent from the Nepalese holy man. Alexis reverently unwrapped the soft kidskin covering, unwound the silken wrap and placed the book on the carpet in front of the fire. Candles were moved to illuminate.

The book was constructed of leather panels, sewn together so as to unfold in eight sections. Alexis pointed to the Sanskrit design on the cover.

"That's the number twenty-four," he said.

"Why twenty-four?" asked Brian.

Alexis smiled enigmatically and flipped open the cover. Each of the eight panels of the leather manuscript was divided into three sections and in each of the 24 panels a picture was inscribed.

The bottom panel was shaded red and contained:
1. An Amoeba with the face of a baby with huge red lips.
2. A Fish with the face of a baby.
3. A Frog with the face of a baby.

The second panel from the bottom was shaded orange and contained the pictures of:
4. A Rodent standing alertly with the face of a two-year-old human child.
5. A Lion with the face of a three-year-old child standing over and pulling a toy away from a small animal with the face of a two-year-old human child.
6. A group of apes swinging from a jungle gym with the faces of five-year-old children.

The third row, shaded yellow, contained these three pictures:
7. A group of Paleolithic Hominids picking up stones. They have the faces of modern seven-year-old children.
8. An eight-year-old child in the body of a neolithic thoughtfully examining a flower.
9. A group of children building a tree house together.

The fourth row, shaded green, contained:
10. Knights on horseback with the faces of teenage kids being watched by court ladies with the faces of teenage girls.
11. A husband and wife with their children standing in front of their house.
12. A million people crowded into an enormous city square all facing and looking up to a velvet balcony.

The fifth row, shaded a rich blue, contained:
13. A beautiful, naked, human, hermaphrodite—the body radiating energy: glowing.
14. A Yogi-naked hermaphrodite radiating, glowing with sense of precise control of the energy.
15. A beautiful woman and man locked in Yab-Yum position radiating and glowing.

The sixth row, shaded light-electric blue, contained:
16. A beautiful naked human hermaphrodite. The brain is visible as are the extensive tendrils of nerves; the body glows.
17. A Yogi—naked hermaphrodite with brain and nervous system visible sending out tendrils of energy that embrace & cre-

ate the surrounding material forms.

18. A series of mountaintops. On each sits a Yogi (as in preceding) with tendrils of nerve signals linking them & energizing the surrounding forms.

The seventh row, shaded violet, contained:

19. A Double Helix intertwined energy coils. Along the strips the preceding 18 forms are portrayed in red.

20. The Double Helix is crowned by the head and face of a Yogi. The Yogi's Brain intertwines the Double Helix.

21. A spaghetti tangle of Double Helices in a spherical form, the whole image radiating like a Star.

The Eighth row, shaded silver, contained:

22. Stars in a velvet Black Sky.

23. Stars that form a Galactic Brain.

24. Strips and spirals of stars infolding to a Central Black Hole.

"What does it say?" asked Brian, pointing to a script on the bottom of the scroll.

Alexis pulled a piece of paper from his pocket and started reading. The candlelight shadowed his noble face. His voice was softly powerful.

"The sequence, that is, the numerical order of evolution is everywhere the same. In the stars, in seed, within the atom, and in the unfolding development of the individual human being.

"Having decoded the numerical sequence which governs the evolution of energy we can use this Periodic Table to decipher evolution at other levels of velocity.

"Some sequences are more easily understood in the evolution of stars. Others are more apparent in the growth and change of seed-forms. Others are most clearly seen in the growth and development of the individual human being going through the changes.

"This parallel study of evolution in the life of stars, in the periodicity of the chemical elements, in the evolution of species on a planet, in individuals popping up at different historical epochs, demonstrates the underlying harmony and overtone-unity of nature and helps the Young Agent discover the similarities in phenomena at all levels of velocity.

"The number of basic principles which govern all processes of change is very small. Let us say there are twenty-four. Different numerical combinations of these twenty-four stages create all the seeming variety of realities that humans can receive.

"The first fundamental rhythm of the universe is polarity. This has been called the law of three. This principle states that every event in the universe is the result of an intersection of three processes: the receptive, the transmitting, and the interacting process between.

"Input. Outgo. Mediated by Integration. Dendrite. Axion. And cell body.

"Black Hole. Big Bang. Transition Between."

"The next fundamental rhythm of the galaxy is the Octave of Change. This has been called the law of 8 (7 + 1).

"Realities consist of vibrations. These vibrations are emitted from every form of structure along the electro-magnetic continuum, proceeding in different directions, crossing one another, colliding, strengthening and weakening one another. DNA fabricates eight brains that deal with eight evolving technologies along the energy continuum. The reason for this eight-phase spectrum can be understood only by any neuro-chemically attuned electronic-age organism. There are eight (7 + 1) colors visible, eight (7 + 1) primary sounds, eight (7 + 1) is the rhythm of the chemical elements.

"Everything is in continual motion moving at fractions and multiples of the speed of light.

Realities consist of vibrations. These vibrations are emitted from every form of structure along the electro-magnetic continuum.

"The natural operational rhythm for the human nervous system is the speed of light, ever-changing. The mind of vibrations is called the In-lightened mind. In-lightenment means thinking at the electrical rate of the Brain. The Brain is the Electrical Body. The Physical Body is the carriage for the Brain, i.e., Body Electric. Human muscular Behavior is the gross, coarse manifestation of faster, stronger nuclear vibrations—charm, charge, strangeness, attractiveness. Each impulse of consciousness from the lower neuro-muscular circuits, when received by the Electrical Body, becomes a small sun radiating meaning. The harmonizing of these innumerable units of experienced light is the skill to be learned by the electronic neurochemical adept."

Alexis stops reading and suddenly turns the book with both hands exposing the other side. With all the panels exposed, the book is about a yard long. Each of the eight panels is a color of the spectrum.

The picture is a vague human-shape, a cloud-like figure in light blue. Within the figure and radiating are golden fibers—it resembles a surrealist anatomical diagram of the human nervous system. The light blue human figure trails off into a network of rainbow swirls and spirals. The effect is startling. The golden-fibers of the nervous system seem to be antennae receiving and vibrating current.

Alexis throws his head up melodramatically and holds his hands out, trembling. His fingers moving as though he were palpating some invisible substance. The others could see crackling current emitting from or being gathered by his hands. He looks at Timothy and smiles. They shift to sit facing each other about five feet apart. Timothy holds up his hands and jumps in surprise.

The number of basic principles which govern all processes of change is very small. Let us say there are twenty-four.

Alexis, Barbara, Brian, Corrine, Timothy, Liz and all the objects in the room are part of a three-dimensional television holograph, in radiant color; everything is constructed of vibrations that flow in fast, smooth rhythm, current alternating so swiftly that a soft texture, infinitely luxuriant, is created. All present are totally joined, indeed, are each part of the holograph, each a shifting pattern of the same field of energy. Each knows what is occurring within the consciousness of the other, could know every thought and experience that the other had ever registered. The sumptuous, voluptuous, mink-lined, rich smoothness of everything—fresh, alive. The "Isness" of Huxley's chair.

Alexis, Brian, Liz, Barbara, Corinne and Tim spend the night in telepathic wave sculpture, imprinting music, absorbing the message of the Nepalese transmission, and watch the sunrise over the mountain. Alexis is now following the Professor like a worshipful, jealous girl, flinging a mink neckpiece over his shoulder.

"What shall I do next?" he asks.

"Find Her. Link up."

"Shall I stay?"

"No. Go now. If you delay here you will be late for our next intersection."

Alexis ceremoniously presents his host with the Nepalese text and leaves with Barbara and Corinne to return to Anita and Keith and Montreux.

[END OF TAPE]

* * * * *

Part 5: OTHER DRUGS

The Ups of Psychedelic Pleasure and the Downs of Narcotic Satisfaction

1979

Hive moralists for millennia have lamented the innate, pervasive tendency of human beings to kick-out in bursts of irrationality and pleasure seeking. Extrasocial self-indulgence. It is important to distinguish between two very different hedonic reactions.

> **Hedonic experiences** caused by activating higher-faster-future brains at the service of—and controlled by—the self. Psychedelic pleasures.
> **Intoxication and narcotic escape experiences** caused by activating slower-lower circuits. Satisfactions.

Both of these experiences take consciousness away from domesticated robothood. Pleasures move one into the post-social, self-actualized future. Up from hive routine. Intoxicants, tranquilizers and narcotics move one back to the past down from domestication, to primate and mammalian instinctual satisfactions.

Civilized terrestrial humans, robotically and blindly harnessed to species tasks, dependent upon gene-hive rewards for duty well done, apparently need to slow-down, turn-off, escape domesticated pressure. Boredom and social inefficiency would result without some sequential opportunity to regress from hive morality, to activate the primitive circuits of the brain. In-toxicants and narcotic escapes are built-in devices to allow ritual regression to earlier, lower, slower stages. Their power and delight is that they are conventionally naughty.

The dutiful Domesticate and the Citizen of the Insectoid State live in a reality centered upon hive duty. More "primitive" brain circuits are still active, but are taboo, often blanked from consciousness. Every successful civilization provides ritualistic means of allowing reactivation of the earlier brains temporarily—naughty immorality, programmed animalism, and permissible retrogression. Brains, as we know, are turned on and off by means of neuro-transmitter chemicals. Each civilization produces ritualistic drug taking that allows temporary animalistic reversion.

This process is best seen in the Japanese culture—surely the most insectoid society in world history. The Japanese have developed ritualistic drunkenness that permits the dutiful Nipponese to regress to animalism. Similarly, alcoholism—abuse of state-manufactured vodka—is tolerated, and even encouraged in the Soviet Union.

It is noteworthy that the German culture, another highly domesticated duty-oriented society, allows its citizens a scheduled intoxication-regression in the Fasching carnival. And even the sober, tidy Swiss permit each other a Springtime return to pseudo-bestiality during which these paragons of domesticated tidy familiarity become tipsy and lurch around like sodden bears, shamelessly littering the streets of Basel with confetti! (Masks are worn at these carnival regressions. The Burghers do not want to have their inner animals seen.)

Other methods for ceremonial return of the animal brain-stages involve totems exhibited at athletic events, parades, and social gatherings. Observe that the unrepressed emotions released at these events are not sexual. Genital satisfaction is not the central motive. Middle age, middle-class folks return to pre-adolescence and become exhibitionistic monkeys or noisy, often savage mammals. Recall South and Central American and European soccer (football) matches in which thousands of spectators engage in physical violence directed against the territorial rival.

An amusing diagnostic sidelight on domesticated terrestrial civilizations: it is acceptable to phone-in sick to the office and thus avoid work.

The orchestrated revival of earlier brains is a basic necessity in any stable gene pool. Each of our evolutionary stages has its own ego, demands activation, and must be allowed to cut loose on some regular basis. The best-run civilizations have worked out a weekly return of the regressed. The domesticate works dutifully Monday through Friday. Saturday she is allowed to assemble in animal-totem competitions—the Bulldogs of Yale versus the Horned Toads of Texas Christian. Saturday night, the socially approved intoxicant is imbibed, permitting a temporary explosion of mammalian territorial competition and sexual low-jinks. Sunday morning the chastened and hung-over domesticate attends a DNA adoration ceremony in which the dignified gene-hive Creator is recognized and the brief foray back to animalism exorcised. The domesticate, purged and reborn, is ready to start the next week of hive duty.

So far we have discussed alcohol, which triggers off mammalian reactions. Another powerful set of neurotransmitters reconstruct even more primitive realities. Narcotics reactivate infant brain experiences and even put the domesticate in touch with relaxed, floating, vegetative pre-terrestrial, marine, womb-neurological realities.

The difference between intoxicant-narcotic behavior and hedonic behavior should now be clear.

Narcotic drugs are approved when used in sickness rituals. Symptomatic cries for help can stimulate shaman-doctors to offer the narcotic experience which activates lower-brain consciousness—ancient, infantile, vegetative. The taboo is necessary to hive discipline. The narcotic return to marine status is so tempting, so inviting, that it must be administered by an authority figure. The domesticate is not allowed access to First Circuit neurotransmitters. Self-administration of narcotics to actualize infantile responses cannot be tolerated for fear that everyone will reject the busy, hectic, adult demands of the hive and escape back to vegetative-ocean bliss. The Doctor Ceremony is the method by which hive-society allows citizens to plug back into the early marine circuits.

An amusing diagnostic sidelight on domesticated terrestrial civilizations: it is acceptable to phone-in sick to the office and thus avoid work. Hive-society recognizes that the insectoid slavery it imposes is basically lethal to the workers. The ceremony of sick leave is allowed.

It is impossible, however, to phone in "well" to the hive-center. To announce: "I feel so good today, I'm not coming in to work." In the hedonic society of the future, provision will be made for "well-leave" in addition to "sick-leave."

The difference between intoxicant-narcotic behavior and hedonic behavior should now be clear. The former engages earlier-slower-lower instinctual brains. The latter moves consciousness and behavior into the self-actualized future, engages future neural circuits. The former are rewards for the overworked domesticate. The latter are genetic endowments, new brains presented, ready-or-not, by the evolutionary process—not earned, but grown into.

THE HEROIN FILES

1966

Have you ever talked to an articulate junkie? The appeal of heroin is the void. The warm, soft cocoon of nothingness. Surcease. Easeful death. The vacuum gamble. The game of the junkie is to nod out. To pass over the line into unconsciousness. The last thought of the junkie as he slips away is, "Have I gone too far this time? Overdose? *Au revoir* or good-bye? ..."

> **To cure the junkie, you must humbly admit that he is a more deeply spiritual person than you, and you accept the cosmic validity of his search to transcend the game.**

It is of interest that the heroin addict and the illuminated Buddha end up at the same place. The void. The junkie is a deeply religious person. Thus our physicians and psychiatrists have no luck in "curing" addicts. If you see an addict as a social misfit, a civic nuisance who must be rehabilitated, you completely miss the point.

To cure the junkie, you must humbly admit that he is a more deeply spiritual person than you, and you accept the cosmic validity of his search to transcend the game, and you help him see that blackout drugs are just bad methodology because you just can't keep holding the "off" switch. The healthier way to visit the void is through psychedelic rather than anesthetic experience.

PRISON

1969

Oh yes, I remember you, Mother Opium, Womb Queen. Pink golden boobs ripening, liquid smile, legs inviting. Sprawled, soft papaya cunt tasseled slender finger opening smooth lips. Oh, do come climb inside my soft cocoon, she murmurs.

And Mistress Alcoholia, the Stupor Queen, wanton, bending forward, saucy face turned over her shoulder. Oh please fuck me rearly. Her round buttocks wiggling, velvet slit whispering, oh now, oh now, honey, you're going to honey fuck my honey ass. Cha cha cha.

And Princess Cocaine, the Go-Go Queen, dancing naked on the shiny crystal tabletop. Her platinum hair swinging, her high heels clacking. Do it to me! Oh do it! Do it to me. Do it! Do it! Do it! Harder! Faster! Harder!

And Mademoiselle Aphrodisia, the Orgasm Queen, her big saucer black eyes smiling, miniskirt pulled up, black stockings, cream thighs, curled black cunt hair spread open murmuring pussy mouth pouting, come, kiss me, come kiss me, make me come, come, come.

The fellow prisoner I have nicknamed "Burroughs" is grinning. "The nervous system feels no pain. With the right dope and good pictures in your head you don't need nothing more. Want some heroin?"

The prisons are filled with heroin vibrations. Junkies involved in the ancient cult devotion to Mother Opium.

I entered prison with a fear of heroin. Logically, I knew that anyone had the right to put anything in his body. But I maintained a moral superiority about junkies. Now I listen to the thoughtful words of men who understand and truly love heroin.

The prisoner I have nicknamed "Burroughs" tells me: "I was making a heroin tantra with this singer, the most elegant user I ever fixed, a heroin with a mind like a looking glass; Lady H herself. We were fixing each other with such gentleness and love, *man*. H in the arm and physeptone in the ass. Identification becomes complete. I can no longer separate the woman from the drug. All was she, every cell in my body whispers Her name. You just got to have respect for Lady H. Like any other woman, she's a goddess when loved but a whore when abused. She's the Sphinx woman, the foxy chick that turns you on so much that you flip so crazy for her that you throw everything away just to be with her.

SWITZERLAND

1972–73 (written 1983)

My experiment with heroin at this time was not the result of alienation and boredom. The two years of enforced exile in Switzerland were hard, but not enough to drive me to the needle.

One factor was the presence of a houseguest, Brian Barritt, British philosopher of junk, and his wife Liz. Although Brian clucked with virtuous disapproval about heroin—just like every other lying junkie—his every word and deed conveyed an intriguing sense of the dark, deep, vegetative wisdom of opium.

Another factor in the environment encouraging heroin experimentation was the Rolling Stones, who were in Montreux in 1972 recording "Exile On Main Street." I used to hang out with Anita and Keith Richards at the baroque villa of Prince Stash de Rolle. Everywhere I went that summer, I heard that low-down beat of the Stones celebrating Sister Morphine and Brown Sugar, singing about his basement room and his needle and his spoon, wailing the profound philosophic thought of the season: "I stuck a needle in my arm. It did some good, it did some harm."

But I had no desire to initiate personal heroin research until destiny floated an enormous supply of the stuff right into my house.

At that time there were about fifty sincere, middle-class hippies in Switzerland and I knew them all. For that matter, I met many of their parents. One of them, Inger, a stewardess for Swiss Air, came by my house looking for Brian. She had purchased a large amount of pure heroin in Beirut just for the lark. She had smuggled it into Zurich and now, a bit flustered, wondered what to do with it.

"Why not take one sniff of it to see what it's like and throw it in the lake," I said.

"Brian would have a heart attack if he missed out on this," said Inger.

> The opiates and other addictive escape-drugs from psychedelic drugs, which increase sensitivity to, and understanding of, the broad spectrum of human realities.

"Here. I'm going to leave some for Brian."

On his return a few days later, Brian sensed the presence of heroin when he was fifty feet away from the house. He pestered me to take it with him as an experiment. I had read most of the books written about heroin, both literary and scientific, but I had only tried it once, with R.D. Laing and Alex Trocchi in London. In spite of my negative bias, I felt well prepared and well-guided for another low-down high.

Brian came to the session in Bombay silk. I put on music, reclined on the cushions, and watched Brian perform his ritual. He dissolved some powder in a spoon, which he heated over a candle. It was agreed that he would go first to establish potency. He loosened his silk scarf from his neck and, holding one end in his left hand, bound the other end around his bicep. By extending his left arm he tightened the scarf until his vein popped up blue and inviting. He shot up.

All this was done with a calm and deliberateness of a surgical ballet. He laid the needle down and fell back on the cushions with a deep sigh of pleasure. A few minutes later he sat up smiling. He said he knew what dosage I would require.

Brian shook his head as he prepared my shot. "I'd hate to be known as the person who got Timothy Leary hooked on heroin."

When the drug hit my vein, I felt the warm flush of euphoria that is worshipped among junkies. No question about it: I felt wonderful for a couple of minutes. For the next half hour, I enjoyed a relaxed noodly bliss, a giggly nonchalance about worldly matters. Soon I fell into heavy sleep.

The next morning Brian was at my door, eager to continue the research. I had no desire for more heroin, so I proposed that we wait until the next night for the next session. The postponement caused a predictable distress in Brian. To avoid the nagging and fidgeting game, I gave him half of the supply, reserving the remainder for what trials I might wish to make at later times.

That night, just before bedtime, I allowed Brain to give me an intramuscular injection. It made me feel mellow and pleasantly somnolent.

The third night of the experiment I sniffed some heroin, and again felt myself sigh in satisfaction.

On the fourth day Brian had run out of his stash. He became irritable. By the time he got around to requesting a hit from mine, I had already flushed it down the toilet.

The opiates and other addictive escape-drugs that lower intelligence have the opposite effect from psychedelic drugs, which increase sensitivity to, and understanding of, the broad spectrum of human realities.

THE ANTIDEPRESSANT FILES

1984

Psychopharmacology, particularly in its use of the tranquilizers, has introduced the notion of "turning off" irrelevant or inappropriate emotion, thus giving medical respectability to the Hindu and hipster notion of being "cool." Let us consider a dictionary definition of emotion: "agitation of the passions or sensibilities often involving physiological changes. Rage, fear, greed, desire, gratitude, jealousy, self-pity." Is this any way to run a species?

1993

Q: I was curious how you feel about the widespread use of the new psychoactive drugs, such as Prozac, for treating conditions other than depression—just for a sort of pick-me-up.

Timothy Leary: In the fifties, we wanted to take the power of diagnosis and treatment away from the medics and put it in the hands of people. In the fifties and sixties we took the power monopoly of psychoactive drugs away from the doctors. I totally deplore the notion of an M.D. giving pills to patients; a medical doctor giving psychological or psychoactive-change agents to another person. It's mechanical. It's factory-like. To say that there is a cure for something called depression—I never thought those categories were scientific. We need to quantify or dimensionalize these things. Instead, we develop *methods of dimensionalizing*: "On a rating scale of one to ten, how depressed are you?" "Well, Jesus, I'm a two right now, but last Tuesday night I was up there with a nine." In other words, when you dimensionalize a human behavior, it's no longer a branded one-dimensional label on your forehead that says you're a Moslem or a Christian or a hysteric or anal—we change from moment to moment, so these identities are not final products.

I still oppose the M.D.s passing out psychoactive drugs to patients and treating them like helpless victims: "Here, open your mouth and let Big Daddy give you a pill."

THE KETAMINE FILES

1979

Neurogenetic theory predicts the discovery of an enzyme found within the nerve cells of dying animals. This chemical, synthesized and administered to healthy subjects under optimal, voluntary conditions, will produce the experience of death with no effect on normal body functions. We hypothesize that the "G-Pill" will suspend space and body imprints, and allow consciousness to tap the final dialogue between the DNA master code and the servant neuron. Then humankind will have an experimental tool for examining what happens when we die. *[Sounds like Ketamine—Editor]*

1995

We have to assume that the best rehearsal for death would involve induction of near-death experiences (NDEs). There's a tremendous body of literature, as well as a vast reservoir of individuals, who can tell you about this experience firsthand.

You can practice the NDE with Ketamine. An intra-muscular injection of 1–2 cc. will do the trick.

Scientists have recently discovered a tremendous similarity between how Ketamine works on brain chemistry and what happens to the brain during NDEs. According to research done by brain researcher Dr. Karl Jansen, conditions that precipitate NDEs release a flood of glutamate, overexciting acting NMDA brain receptors. This can produce brain damage. Ketamine prevents this over-excitation. Apparently, the brain produces its own Ketamine-like brain chemicals that bind to NMDA receptors under near-death conditions and protect the brain cells. Given the similarities between reported Ketamine experiences and NDEs, it seems that the altered-state experience is triggered by the action of this substance defending the brain cells from the onrushing glutamate. Also, according to Jansen, "mounting evidence suggests that the reproduction/induction of NDEs by Ketamine is not simply an interesting coincidence. Exciting new discoveries include the major binding site for Ketamine on brain cells, known as the phencyclidine (PCP) binding site of the NMDA receptor, the importance of NMDA receptors in the cerebral cortex, particularly in the temporal and frontal lobes, and the key role of these sites in cognitive processing, memory, and perception.

"NMDA receptors play an important role in epilepsy, psychosis, and in producing the cell death that results from a lack of oxygen, a lack of blood, and from epileptic fits (excito-toxicity). This form of brain cell damage can be prevented by administration of Ketamine."

Ketamine produces an out-of-body experience that often involves feelings of floating, sometimes through a tunnel. Ego loss is more absolute than with the other psychedelics at high-dosage levels. Some experimenters report the sense that there is no self present having this experience—just the pure light/information space itself. On Ketamine, one senses a thin film between this world and the next. And it's not scary. There tends to be none of the psychological content and less potential for panic with Ketamine than one finds when experiencing other forms of psychedelic dying. One truly does not care too much about the world left behind during the Ketamine event.

* * * * *

CHAPTER FOUR
THE POLITICS OF ECSTASY & INFAMY

THE FIRST DRUG BUSTS
1994

"I made you, Adam, to be in my likeness, and I put you in the ultimate tourist destination, The Garden of Eden. I'm also giving you a mate—a little kitchen slave named Eve. *Boy...* you can do whatever you want, except for these two food and drug regulations. See that tree over there? That's the Tree of Immortality. It offers genetic rejuvenation and cloning. You shall not eat of the fruit of that lest you become a God like me and live forever. You see that tree over there? That's even more dangerous. You shall not eat of the fruit of that because that is the Tree of Knowledge. It offers expansions of consciousness."

Genesis makes it clear that the whole universe is owned, operated, controlled, and fabricated by one God and he's a big, bad-tempered male.

BUST & COURTROOM NOTES
1965 (written 1983)

Leary was busted several times during the 1960s and 1970s and spent four years in prison and two years in exile. While the narrative of this ordeal took over his life from the middle of the 1960s until the middle of the 1970s, if I were to try to present the story here, it would take over the entire book. Here are just a few fragments, related to the charges for his first bust in Laredo, Texas and the second, a trial scene that would be the start of a 1970s "Spy vs. Spy" adventure story that would involve a prison escape, the Weather Underground and Black Panthers, wealthy European confidence men, Interpol, The Nixon White House, the CIA, and a cat-and-mouse game with the FBI that remains controversial to this day.—*Editor*

Bail was set at $100,000. For $10 worth of weed! On the way back to the jail, a guard gave me the name of the best bail bondsman in town, who happened to be waiting for us at the jail. He, in turn, gave me the name of the best lawyer in town, who showed up immediately.

The lawyer was reassuring about our release on bail. I had about $3,000 in cash and he miraculously worked it out so that we still had enough money for tickets to New York after paying him and the bondsman.

But he was not optimistic about the long-range prospects. Rosemary and Jack would walk free. He was sure the Grand Jury couldn't indict them. Susan, because of her age, would get probation, and her record would be expunged when she reached the age of 21. But I was in trouble. The US Attorney in Houston was flying down a crew of prosecutors and investigators. Obviously, it was a big case for them. The way they were encouraging publicity suggested that they wanted to make an example of me. I had to realize that people down here in southern Texas were a bit more conservative than the people up around Harvard. The federal judge for this circuit was an old tiger named Connally, notoriously tough on northerners coming through Laredo with marijuana. It would be hard to get a sympathetic jury in a small town like this. Best thing was to make a deal, my attorney added. "You might end up doing four months' jail time with probation. A lot depends on a repentant attitude in cases of this sort."

"Repentant?" I said indignantly. "What does that mean?"

"Oh—you make public statements denouncing drugs."

"For a pinch of marijuana that wasn't actually mine? Four months in the slammer. Probation. No way! This whole thing is a set up and a frame. I'm going to fight it."

The lawyer dropped his head and studied his lap. "I must tell you that the case against you is nonexistent. The contraband belonged to Rosemary and was in Susan's possession. You have nothing to do with it legally. You obviously didn't know the stuff was in the car because you wouldn't have crossed the border to customs. Right? All you have to do is tell the truth and you'll walk free."

"But then Susan and Rosemary would take the fall."

"The court isn't going to hit them hard. Susan's a minor. And Rosemary's a poor confused misguided girl under your influence. If she cries and promises the judge to be good in the future, I'll get her off with probation."

"But I'm not some criminal looking for loopholes. I'd feel immoral, like I was copping out."

Obviously, it was a big case for them. The way they were encouraging publicity suggested that they wanted to make an example of me.

The lawyer let loose a string of colorful Texan oaths invoking rattlesnakes' genitals and lizards' eliminative organs. "Every time I hear a client talk about moral principles, I know I'm going to lose the case and not get paid enough for the headaches. You don't understand how much trouble you can get into. If you take responsibility for the contraband, there's no way we can keep you out of jail."

"What about appeals? I'll take this to the Supreme Court. Everyone knows the marijuana law is an unconstitutional tax statute. Marijuana's not a narcotic. We'll get that Mickey Mouse statute thrown out."

"I know. I've heard several hundred people sitting in that very chair say the same thing. And they all come around in the end and make a deal. You're talking about several years of expensive litigation, $100,000 minimum. That marijuana law has been around for a long time. And keep in mind that only one in every 200 cases is accepted for Supreme Court review. You can probably stay out of jail during the review process on appeal bond, but you'll still be a convicted criminal. If you do anything they don't like—get arrested again, say something publicly that displeases them—your bail can be revoked and you'll be in prison while your case works its way up the courts. If you fight the charges, then you'll get hit with all three felony counts. They add up to a lot of prison time."

"How much?"

"Let's see. Twenty years for smuggling, five-year mandatory minimum. Another 20 for transportation. That also carries a 5-year mandatory minimum. And up to 10 years for the tax count. So you're talking a mandatory minimum of 10 years, and if they're really mad at you, as I gather they are, up to 50 years. Plus a $50,000 fine."

"I could go to prison for life for $10 of marijuana that wasn't my own?"

The lawyer looked down on his papers unhappily. "It's terrible, I know. All I can do is get you the best deal available. This system is pretty set in its ways. I wouldn't advise you to fight it."

I sat silently, assimilating information that was going to change forever the way I understood and related to society.

"Anyway, we don't have to make any decisions right now," said the lawyer. "It will be several months before we go to trial. You can get other opinions. I'll get you bailed out tonight."

The jailer escorted me back to my cell, and I heard that sound of iron gates closing again. It was dark in the cell. I sat on the bunk and thought.

Here it was. A moment of political truth. My Laredo lawyer said it: "They want to make an example of you." Well, I'd make an example of them. I couldn't plead guilty because I felt no guilt. And I couldn't lie about the harmlessness of giggly little marijuana. I couldn't throw myself on the mercies of a crusty old Texas judge and Texas probation officers.

I wasn't going to submit passively to the role of scapegoat, the Harvard psychologist who got into that trouble over drugs. Liberty was at stake here, freedom of access to your own body and brain; a right I believed was protected by the Constitution. Sitting in a dark jail cell on Christmas Eve, 1965, flushed with virtuous indignation about the wickedness of the marijuana laws, I resolved to fight this case in the courts of the land, to mobilize legal teams, to devise courtroom tactics, to fight appeals, motions, briefs, depositions, to speak in defense of the rights of American citizens to manage their own bodies and brains.

The fatal word in this naïve program was "fight." The adversary nature of the judicial process has never been favorable to philosophers and scientists. Would I choose this arena of battle again? I don't know. It was a stage that I had to go through. And go through it I did.

January 1970 (written 1983)

I find everything about courtrooms dreary and unscientific. Richard Alpert shook his head sympathetically when he came to my trial. "The courtroom is the worst forum for new ideas," he sighed. "Galileo lost. Giordano Bruno got the hot seat. Scopes lost in Tennessee defending evolution. The Jews and Italians threw the book at Jesus for preaching love, while the crook Barabbas got off. There's a 2,000-year-old public relations lesson for philosophers there."

"Now you tell me," I replied.

The jury did not give out promising signals. Orange County, home turf of Richard Nixon and the John Birch Society. My twelve peers were sternly conservative in dress and demeanor. The evidence brought against me included the arresting officer's two weather-beaten roaches and a few flakes of marijuana, vacuumed from the pocket of a jacket found in the front seat of the station wagon. I could have taken the stand and denied possession of the two roaches, truthfully, and perhaps, convincingly. By introducing the seven flakes of cannabis, the state was admitting the flimsiness of the case against me. We had an ex-District Attorney ready to testify that the arresting officer was known to use illegal tactics in making arrests.

Liberty was at stake here, freedom of access to your own body and brain; a right I believed was protected by the Constitution.

Against Rosemary and Jack, however, there were more convincing exhibits—some grass, hashish, and a few acid tabs found on their persons. The DA made it clear that if I were found innocent, an example would be made of Rosemary and Jack. Once again, my attorneys rested the case without putting up any defense. I'd be free on appeal bond again and we'd win in the higher courts, said the lawyers.

On the weekend before the case went to the jury, we returned to the ranch and found our cabin burned down. Ed May, our friend and ranch manager, had run into the blazing building with a wet towel over his head, blindly grabbing the Buddha statue that Peggy Hitchcock had brought to the Newton Center house a few years before. The same week, Fang, our oldest doggy friend, disappeared. A mountain lion or hunters' guns.

On the morning that the case went to the jury, the local paper, *The Santa Anna* appeared with the blood-curdling banner headline: "DRUG-CRAZED HIPPIES SLAY MOTHER AND CHILDREN." An army medical officer named McDonald reported that his home had been invaded by a band of longhaired young people who brutally murdered his wife and children and beat up the doctor. Just so that no one missed the point, they scrawled on the wall in blood: "ACID IS GROOVY. KILL THE PIGS." (Many people sensed immediately that this curious story was a phony. Several years later Doctor McDonald was convicted of this crime, as horrible as the Manson murders.) It was not a good time to get a fair trial on a drug charge. It was not a good time to be a public figure identified with LSD.

The jury came back with the verdict: we were all guilty of the wizard crime, possession.

Then the judge pulled the shocker. I was remanded to jail immediately without appeal bond—unheard of and clearly unconstitutional. The shaved head of his honor glistened under the fluorescent lights as he quoted from an article I had written for "Playboy" magazine ridiculing the marijuana laws.

"For you we throw away the keys," said the jailer as the steel doors slammed shut.

1979

I got involved in a little contest in the 1960s. A minor thing, just a simple genetic Super Bowl competition for the consciousness of a small planet. East versus West. Past versus Future. Washington Senators versus the California Angels. As High Scorer for the Angels, I got put in the penalty box for four years.

NEUROLOGICAL LIBERTY

1967

The problems posed by new ways of changing consciousness, I think, require two new commandments:

> **1: Thou shalt not alter the consciousness of thy fellow man by electrical or chemical means.** Can you change a man's consciousness if he wants you to? Can you teach him how? Yes, but the control of the method has got to be given to the man who owns that brain.

> **2: Thou shalt not prevent thy fellow man from changing his consciousness by electrical or chemical means.** If someone, in altering his consciousness, wreaks clear harm to society, only then can you prevent him. In every such case, the burden of proof must be on society to demonstrate harm before society intervenes.

[In the 1980s, Leary added a new law. Thou shalt not use the phrase "thou shalt not."—*Editor*

1978

Neurophysical Freedom is the freedom to expand, accelerate, and control one's own nervous system and to broadcast and receive electronically. The freedom to migrate from the planet. The constraint against interfering with the brain-reward processes and the neuro-electrical transception of others. The constraint against interfering against the biological choices of others—

genetic self-manipulation, abortion, the right to die, personal sexual and gender selection, and so forth.

THE WAR AGAINST CERTAIN DRUGS

How the South Invaded the North
1986

The popularity of psychedelic drugs is an example of the revival of southern (south of the USA) culture.

Notice that the neurotransmitters illegal in Reagan's land are southern vegetables: the poppy, ground-up coca leaves, the flowering top of the marijuana plant. None of these botanical substances are as physically, or psychologically, dangerous as the factory-made, northern, mind-benders: distilled liquor, North Carolina-grown nicotine and the prescription euphoria and tranqs used legally by middle-class housewives. The southern botanicals—grass, opium, coca—are threatening to the order and conformity demanded by the Factory Culture.

1: These vegetables grow wild. They are non-domesticated. Grown up in mountains, they are hard to control. They are sold on the black market—that naughty unauthorized free exchange that operates outside the control of white bankers and the feudal tax collectors. Inexpensive, wild, southern herbs are the subversive fellow travelers that came with the lucrative slave and rum trades that made our Puritan ancestors wealthy.

2: Native drug rituals are immoral, i.e. banned as sinful by the northern religions. Damn right they are! They incite personal freedoms, pagan celebrations, self-expression, disordered joy, sensual pleasure. They dramatically threaten the control of the priests. Remember those scandalous biblical stories about Moses and the other high-ranking priests coming down the mountain and finding the tribes stoned, whooping it up around the Golden Calf and other natural icons? Heresy. Sin. Devil Worship.

3: The ingestion of native plants is also criminal. Why? Because the white men who write the laws and run the police stations say so!

4: The ingestion of natural plants is not only immoral, criminal, and bad-for-business, it is treasonous. It figures, doesn't it? You are a self-respecting native and in comes these weirdo, white robots, brandishing guns, despoiling your neighborhood, your culture, breaking up your family, scorning your gods. Now the most effective, nonviolent act of political resistance is to perform your native rituals. Get high with a native opium pipe and you and your friends have gently and delightfully floated outside the white man's economic, religious, legal, and political domination.

For centuries, the northern colonists ignored and tolerated the cultivation and ingestion of neuron-botanicals as long as this was restricted to the native quarters. Let the illiterate wags get their primitive kicks. Keep 'em nodding out and blissed.

But in the 1960s, the new postwar generations of white folks began turning away from the Cold War and life on the assembly line. The cultural revolution in America produced a vigorous renaissance of the source religions of the south. Pantheist love of nature was expressed—as was ecological awareness. Worship of bodily grace manifested in physical fitness. High pagan style became hip-high fashion.

The acculturalization of psychedelic drugs by Americans in the 1960s provides a powerful endorsement of tropical religious rituals. The psychedelic drugs are all derived from tropical plants. Psilocybin from mushrooms, mescaline from peyote, LSD from rye-ergot, and, of course, marijuana. These are not the euphoriants, or energizers, or intoxicants favored by urban dwellers. Psychedelics produce states of possession, trance, expanded consciousness, spiritual illumination—powerful, mystical empathies with natural forces. These experiences, which are the aim of ancient pagan religion, are the worst nightmares of the organized religions.

The Reagan Drug War
1990

The counterculture revolution started in 1966, virtually took over the mainstream in 1976, and hit the wall with a thud! in 1980 with the election of Nancy Reagan.

During the 1980s, the gentle, androgynous tolerance of the counterculture was replaced by a hard-on Marine Corps attitude. The pacifism of "Give Peace a Chance" gave way to a swaggering militarism. The conquest of Grenada. The glorious bombing of Qaddafi's tent. The covert war against Nicaragua. Star Trek gave way to Star Wars.

The War on Drugs made mellow marijuana prohibitively expensive. The DEA made sure that the peaceable, visionary elixirs like 'shrooms, Mescaline, LSD, and MDMA became inaccessible. So good-bye to turn on, tune in, drop out . . . and hello to the motto of the 1980s: Hang on. Hang in. Hang over.

And what did the War on Drugs produce? A booze epidemic. Alcohol—the drug of choice of the NRA and the Bubba hunting crowd, along with the American Legion, is back in the saddle.

Turn down! Time out! Throw up!

And cocaine. An epidemic of toot, snort, snow, blow, base, crack has the inner cities wired and fired. Cocaine, the drug that fueled Hitler's SS and the Nazi Blitzkrieg, is turning the inner cities of Reagan-Bush America into battlegrounds! Guns, rifles, and automatic weapons. You can't buy ecstasy in Reagan's America, but you can easily buy guns. Just walk up and name your weapon, Bucko. No questions asked.

Turn out! Shoot up! Drop dead!

And here's a pharmaceutical plus for the post-countercultural America; what unique new Rambo drug rose to prominence during the stand-tall, muscle-bound Reagan-Bush regime that replaced the wimpy Carter years?

Steroids!

Turn off! Tune out! Pump up!

Thanks a lot, Nancy.

There was a reason for this unprecedented escalation in this so-called war. The Reagan hawks were armed to the teeth; all dressed up in uniforms, but had nowhere to go. So, once again, the *nomenclature* fell back on the old stand-by: a Civil War. A jihad against an insidious domestic enemy corrupting us from within.

The new scapegoat victims? The perverted smokers of the Assassin of Youth, the killer weed.

The Holy War Against Self-Medication

During the Democratic administration of 1976–80, fourteen states decriminalized marijuana, and President Carter announced his intention to do the same at the federal level. Carter also did his best to promote civil and human rights.

Shortly after the Grand Old Party assumed power in 1980, the standard belligerent nationalism ploy was dusted off. The Cold War against the Evil Empire was re-declared. Military budgets and the national deficits suddenly lurched toward all-time peaks. But the Soviet Union under Gorbachev wouldn't play the game, and the threats from Iran-Qaddafi-Grenada-Central America were too feeble to justify a war economy.

So the Civil War card was played. A Holy War on Vegetables was declared. Illegal herbs were denounced as "cancers," moral plagues, lethal threats to national security. Politicians of both parties immediately fell into line, and the media, sensing circulation boosts and an audience hungry for moral outrage, scrambled to dramatize the menace.

There was no debate. No rational public discussion about the wisdom of waging a Civil War against some thirty million fellow-Americans who knew from experience that grass is less dangerous than booze. No questions about the common-sense practicality of violating that most basic frontier of liberty, the body and the brain.

Children were applauded for turning in their parents. Fill the prisons. Hang the peddlers. Urine tests for civilian workers. When marijuana arrests reached *five hundred thousand a year,* Nancy Reagan's Civil Warriors were far outstripping the Inquisition's witch-hunts.

And still no audible protests against this blatant fascism! Why were the ACLU and the civil rights movement silent? Where was Amnesty International? Where were the libertarian traditions of this land of freedom?

Critics of the War On Drugs

Three recently published books deal brilliantly with the evils and absurdities of the War on Drugs. These are:

Dealing with Drugs: Consequences of Government Control
ed. Ronald Hanowy. Lexington Books, 1987.

Breaking the Impasse In the War on Drugs
by Steven Wisotsky. Greenwood Press, 1986.

Why We Are Losing the Great War on Drugs and Radical Proposals That Could Make America Safe Again
by Arnold Trebach. Macmillan, 1987.

Dealing with Drugs is a collection of essays by ten distinguished university scholars who demonstrate with fact and logic that the "war on drugs" is futile, harmful, irrational, immoral and illegal.

Professor Hanowy's collection concludes with a magnificent essay, "The Morality of Drug Controls." The author, psychiatrist Thomas Szasz, is one of the most important intellectuals of our times. For thirty years Szasz has brought to the dark, swampy field of psychiatry the same penetrating social logic and laser-sharp morality that Noam Chomsky has given to linguistics and politics. And more, because Dr. Szasz adds a certain down-to-earth, humanist common sense. He writes here, not about drugs, but about drug control as a moral issue, the "drug user" as scapegoat: "I believe that just as we regard freedom of speech and religion as fundamental rights, so should we regard freedom of self-medication as a fundamental right; and that instead of mendaciously opposing or mindlessly promoting illicit drugs, we should, paraphrasing Voltaire, make this maxim our rule: I disapprove of what you take, but I will defend to the death your right to take it."

So the Civil War card was played. A Holy War on Vegetables was declared.

Breaking the Impasse in the War On Drugs is a carefully researched, chilling account of the incalculable damages wrought upon our country and our southern neighbors by the Reagan regime's "war on cocaine." Long sections describe the assault on justice and civil liberties, the growth of big brotherism; the corrosion of the work ethic, the corruption of public officials, disrespect for the law, the international pathology of the War on Drugs, instability and narco-terrorism—the drug-problem problem.

Arnold Trebach, the author of *Why We Are Losing the Great War on Drugs and Radical Proposals That Could Make America Safe Again,* examines in scholarly fashion the failures, the hypocrisies, the corruptions, and the repressive illegalities of the Holy War, and presents fourteen common sense, practical, compassionate "peaceful compromises." Trebach goes behind the grim statistics to address the personal, human side of the conflict: interviews with—and case histories of—the victims: young people kidnapped by their own misguided parents; moderate, intelligent users harshly penalized; cancer, AIDS and glaucoma patients prevented from using appropriate medication; street addicts caught in a system that treats them as criminals rather than as patients.

In the three books discussed, a total of twenty experts in the field agree that legal energy-mood-anesthetic drugs—booze, nicotine, pills—are certainly as disabling and abusive as their illegal counterparts: heroin, marijuana, cocaine. They come to the common-sense conclusion that by decriminalizing and regulating the latter, we could reduce the "drug problem" in one day, from a fatal social cancer to a treatable health annoyance.

The War On Psychedelics

The most pernicious and hypocritical aspect of the current drug situation is the criminalizing of marijuana and psychedelic plants and drugs. Used with a minimum of common sense, marijuana, LSD, mescaline, and psilocybin are valuable tools for exploring the brain and changing the mind. "Psychedelic" means mind expanding. These vegetable products are the very opposite of the "opiate anesthetics," in that they produce hypersensitivity to external sensations and accelerated thought processing. They are not addictive. They have almost no effect on physiology. They change consciousness. They are information drugs. They have been used for millennia in religious ceremonies. Because they alter consciousness in such intense, individual ways, group rituals develop to support and protect the visionary experience. They are rarely used alone, because solitary visions create solipsistic "space-outs."

Psychedelic vegetables when used with optimum regard for "set and setting" are arguably the safest food substances that human beings can ingest. They obviously represent an ancient symbiosis between the sexual organs of flowering plants and the nervous systems of mammals, to the mutual benefit of all concerned.

Therefore, in the struggle for liberty, I suggest a new motto: JUST SAY KNOW!

Since the dawning of the information age in 1946, these psychedelic plants have become extremely popular in regions where cybernetic-digital technologies—television, computers—have taken over. In the last twenty years, the influence of psychedelic drugs on art, music, literature, fashion, language, electronic graphics, film, television commercials, holistic medicine, science, theoretical mathematics, computers, ecological awareness, and esoteric spiritual and philosophical exploration has been so pervasive that it has become invisible.

It is interesting that the Drug-War crusaders rarely mention psychedelic substances. Government experts and *Newsweek* editors rave and writhe about the dangerous pleasures of cocaine, the irresistible ecstasies of crack, the addictive seductions of heroin. One hit of these siren substances, they trumpet, and you're a slave to their power. But they never discuss the reasons why millions of non-addicts prefer to use marijuana or magic mushrooms, or the benign and gentle MDMA (Ecstasy). The law-enforcement doctors mumble about "gateway" drugs and let it go at that. That which you cannot demonize—"killer weed"—must be systematically ignored. The tactic is the familiar fear-fight line. Hey! This is no time for logical, academic discussions or treasonous undermining of the war effort! It's an all-out conflict between good and evil! The Demon Foe has our backs to the wall!

It is interesting that the authors of those three logical, scientific, libertarian books discussed above, do not deal with the positive aspects of the psychedelic drugs, nor do they refer to the hundreds of scientific papers about the benefits, personal and cultural, that can occur if these drugs are used with prudence and planning. They are not psychologists or humanist philosophers, after all. Thank God!

With calm unanimity, these gentlemen come on as sober, rational academics. The attitude is magisterial, almost judicial. They express not one dot of approval for the use of mind-changing substances, legal or illegal. They condemn intoxication. They are opposed to the War on Vegetables only because it is futile and aggravates the problem. Occasionally, they sigh in regret for the human weaknesses that lead people to seek change or solace in drugs—it appears unlikely that any of these prudent academics has ever been high. Their prescription is simple: Substitute government regulation and education for repression.

I enthusiastically applaud this statesmanly approach. It could work in Belfast, the Middle East, Afghanistan, and here in our own Civil War on Drugs.

Once again, we are reminded that the only solution to human problems is intelligent thought and accurate, open communication.

Therefore, in the struggle for liberty, I suggest a new motto: JUST SAY KNOW!

CONVERSATION WITH WILLIAM S. BURROUGHS

1991

Timothy Leary: Let's talk about the Drug War hysteria.

William S. Burroughs: Just a couple of tips—something that nobody has gone into, in this whole drug debate, is the simple fact that before the Harrison Narcotics Act in 1914, all these drugs were sold across the counter.

TL: Opium? Cocaine?

WSB: Opium, cocaine, morphine, heroin... sold over the counter. These were the days that the conservatives now evoke as "the good old days." Was America floundering? Of course not. And look at how well the English system of dealing with addicts worked, until the "American Brain Commission" went over there and talked them out of it. When I was there in 1967 and took the apomorphine cure with Dr. Dent, there were about six hundred addicts in the U.K., all of them registered and known because they could obtain their heroin quite legally. You could get cocaine too. Now that they've made it impossible, and the doctors can't prescribe to addicts, God knows how many addicts they have. And, of course, narcotics agents.

TL: Switzerland is interesting. They have parks in Zurich and other places where junkies can go. The attitude is humanistic: "We're one family; we're all Swiss. And if our junkies want to shoot up, we'll provide clean needles." There's no criminality involved.

WSB: I remember at one point I was at one of these Dutch places where they had needles and works; you put a coin in a thing and out came the needle.

TL: Works-o-matics.

WSB: Works-o-matics! Anyway, if you look at the history, the fact is that for years there was no British heroin problem. The system worked very well.

TL: Well, the problem is the Puritan, Cromwellian moralists who have always tried their best to impose their f**** neuroses on America and England. Any sort of pleasure, or any sort of idea that the individual has a right to pursue happiness, and they're after you. It's basically inquisitional . . . religious. I blame the Puritans.

THE TRAGIC AFFAIR OF MARY PINCHOT & THE PSYCHEDELIC PRESIDENT 1962–1976 (written 1983)

Winter 1962

While sitting at my desk, I looked up to see a woman leaning against the doorpost, hip tilted provocatively, studying me with a bold stare. She appeared to be in her late 30s. Good looking. Flamboyant eyebrows, piercing, green-blue eyes, fine-boned face. Amused, arrogant, aristocratic. "Dr. Leary," she said coolly. "I've got to talk to you."

She took a few steps forward and held out her hand. "I'm Mary Pinchot. I've come from Washington to discuss something very important. I want to learn how to run an LSD session."

"That's our specialty here. Would you like to tell me what you have in mind?"

"I have found this friend who's a very important man. He's impressed by what I've told him about my own LSD experiences and what other people have told him. He wants to try it himself. So I'm here to learn how to do it. I mean, I don't want to goof up or something."

"Why don't you have your important friend come here with you to look over our project for a couple of days? Then if it makes sense to all concerned, we'll run a session for him."

Don't you think that if a powerful person were to turn on with his wife or girlfriend it would be good for the world?

"Out of the question. My friend is a public figure. It's just not possible."

"People involved in power usually don't make the best subjects."

"Look," said Mary Pinchot, "I've heard Allen Ginsberg on radio and TV shows saying that if Khrushchev and Kennedy would take LSD together they'd end world conflict. Isn't that the idea—to get powerful men to turn on?"

"Allen says that, but I've never agreed. Premier Khrushchev should turn on with his wife in the comfort and security of his Kremlin bedroom. Same for Kennedy."

"Don't you think that if a powerful person were to turn on with his wife or girlfriend it would be good for the world?"

"Nothing that involves brain-change is certain. But in general, we believe that for anyone who's reasonably healthy and happy, the intelligent thing to do is to take advantage of the multiple realities available to the human brain."

"Do you think that the world would be a better place if men in power had LSD experiences?"

"Look at the world," I said. "Nuclear bombs proliferating. More and more countries run by military dictators. No political creativity. It's time to try something, *anything* new and promising."

I offered her some California sherry from a half-gallon jug, but she made a cute little face and invited me out for champagne. She continued asking me questions as we sat in the cocktail lounge. When I rose to go back to my office, she invited me to have dinner. I suggested that she come along to Newton Center to eat at my house, where the kids were waiting. When we walked in, Malaca flashed a hostile glance at Mary, then recovered and greeted her with her French-accented charm.

We never got to eat. Michael Hollingshead mixed drinks, got a bit tipsy and started lecturing about brain drugs. Mary helped Malaca and me prepare dinner for the kids, and later we four took a low dose of mushrooms and sat around the fire. Michael was in top form, acting out high spots of former sessions. Behind his wild comedy, he was teaching Mary about the problems of inner navigation: how to deal with them, how to center yourself, how to avoid panic, how to locate handholds of comforting reality.

Then I saw her face go tense.

"You poor things," she murmured. "You have no idea what you've gotten into. You don't really understand what's happening in Washington with drugs, do you?"

"We've heard some rumors about the military," I said.

"It's time you learned more. The guys who run things—I mean the guys who *really* run things in Washington—are very interested in psychology, and drugs in particular. These people play hardball, Timothy. They want to use drugs for warfare, for espionage, for brainwashing, for control."

"Yes," I said. "We know about that."

"But there are people like me who want to use drugs for peace, not for war, to make people's lives better. Will you help us?"

"How?"

"I told you. Teach us how to run sessions… use drugs to do good."

Even though we were glowing in that pleasant conspiratorial feeling of those who are sharing a psychedelic session, imprinting each other with positive feelings, I felt uneasy. There was something calculating about Mary, that tough hit you get from people who live in the hard political world.

I asked once again, "Who are these friends of yours who want to use drugs for peace?"

"Women," she said laughing. "Washington, like every other capital city in the world, is run by men. These men who conspire for power can only be changed by women. And you're going to help us."

I drove Mary to the airport the next day and loaded her with books and papers about our research.

"I don't think you're quite ready to start running sessions," I told her.

"I agree. I'll be back soon for more practice. And don't forget," she said. "The only hope for the world is intelligent women."

Fall 1962

One fall afternoon I received a phone call from Mary Pinchot, my mysterious visitor from Washington. "Can you meet me right away in Room 717, Ritz Hotel?"

At the door I paused to smooth my shirt and my trousers and handbrush my hair. Enchanting as before, she motioned to a silver ice bucket with a bottle of Dom Perignon tilting out. "I'm here to celebrate," she said.

I twisted the bottle to make the cork pop gently. "Your hush-hush love affair is going well?"

"Oh yes. Everything is going beautifully. On all fronts, in fact. I can't give details, of course. But *top* people in Washington are turning on. You'd be amazed at the sophistication of some of our leaders. And their wives. We're getting a little group together, people who are interested in learning how to turn on."

"Really. I thought politicians were too power-oriented."

"You must realize, implausible as it may seem, there are a lot of very smart people in Washington. Especially now—with this administration. Power is important to them. And these drugs do give a certain power. That's what it's all about. Freeing the mind."

She held out her glass for more champagne. "Until very recently, control of American consciousness was a simple matter for the guys in charge. The schools instilled docility. The radio and TV networks poured out conformity."

The only hope for the world is intelligent women.

"No doubt about it," I agreed.

"You may not know that dissident organizations in academia are also controlled. The CIA controls some of the radical journals and student organizations and runs them with deep-cover agents."

"Oh come on, Mary," I said. "That sounds pretty paranoid to me."

Mary sipped at her glass and shook her head. "I hate to be the one to break the news to you. Do you remember the American Veterans Committee, that liberal GI group you belonged to after the war? The CIA started that. Just like Teddy Roosevelt started the American Legion after the First World War. Remember your liberal friend Gilbert Harrison? He ran the radicals out of AVC. And later he bought the *New Republic*—that so-called progressive magazine—from Michael Straight, your hero. Do you know why Michael Straight backed Henry Wallace for President in 1948? To siphon liberal votes away from Truman."

"How do you know all this? How did you know I knew Michael Straight?"

"I knocked you with those facts to get your attention. It's a standard intelligence trick. I could tell you hundreds of little stories like that."

She held out her glass again. I filled it, then drained and refilled my own. My head was spinning.

"And guess what these guys are most interested in right now?"

"Drugs, I suppose."

"You got it. A few years ago, they became absolutely obsessed with the notion that the Soviets and the Chinese were persuading our POWs in Korea to defect by brainwashing them with LSD and mescaline."

"That's certainly possible. With what we've discovered about set and setting, we know that almost anyone's mind can be changed in any direction."

"Any direction?"

"With a minimum of information about the subject's personal life and two or three LSD sessions, you could get the most conventional person to do outrageous things."

"Suppose the person wanted to be brainwashed in a certain direction... wanted to change himself?"

"Easier yet. Our research is conclusive on this. Changing your mind, developing a new reality-fix, is a simple and straightforward proposition. Of course, altering your mind is one thing. Changing the outside world to conform to your new vision remains the difficult problem for us..." I struggled for a word, "...us utopiates."

Mary clapped her hands together like a birthday girl. "Utopiates! Beautiful. That's what it's all about, isn't it? Make it a better world." She sat down next to me and held my hand.

"Let's make a deal, as one utopiate to another. I'll tell you some things about you that are very important and then you'll tell me the same."

"What do you want to know?"

She laughed. "Let me start off. Since drug research is of vital importance to the intelligence agencies of this country, you'll be allowed to go on with your experiments as long as you keep it fairly quiet. You are doing exploratory work the CIA tried to do in the 1950s. So they're more than happy to have you do their research for them. As long as it doesn't get out of hand."

"What do you mean by 'out of hand'?"

"Timothy, think. You're involved in the Big Game here. Mind-change is the key to power. They'll deal with you about the same way the Soviets would handle a nuclear physicist with liberal, libertarian ideals. They'll indulge your utopian fantasies. They know that creative scientists tend to be freethinkers. They'll run you with a loose silken cord as long as you don't stir up the masses."

"OK, I'll try not to stir up the masses. And what can I do for you?"

"I told you the first time we met. I want to learn how to brainwash."

"That doesn't sound very ladylike."

At this she burst into laughter. "If I can teach the use of utopiates to the wives and mistresses of important people in our government, then we can... well shit, Timothy, don't you see what we can do?"

"What?"

"We can do on a bigger scale what you are already doing with your students—use these drugs to free people. For peace, not war. We can turn on the Cabinet. Turn on the Senate. The Supreme Court. Do I have to explain further?"

Her proposal was very scary. But come to think of it, it was close to what we Harvardites, in our session rooms, lazily architecturing hopeful futures, had spelled out as the goal of psychedelic research.

I looked at myself in the reflection of the window: a 42-year-old man being lured into a feminist plot to turn on the leaders of the United States government to world peace through psychedelic drugs. She lay on the bed, pleased with herself, awaiting my reaction, knowing I was going to agree.

"OK. What do you want from me? The drugs?"

"Just a little bit to get started. With our connections we'll be able to get all the supplies we want. And all you need too. Mainly I want advice about how to run sessions and how to handle any problems that come up."

We spent the next four hours in a cram course on psychedelic sessions. Set and setting. Centering. Room service brought more champagne and then dinner. I drove her to Logan to get a night flight back to Washington. The next day I mailed off a stack of session reports. Since she had sworn me to secrecy, I told no one except Michael Hollingshead.

Mexico 1963

One thing that didn't happen in Mexico 1963 was an expected visit from Mary Pinchot. I received a short cryptic note, postmarked Washington, DC typed and unsigned.

> PROGRAM GOING VERY WELL HERE. EXTREMELY
> WELL!!! HOWEVER, I WON'T BE JOINING YOU. TOO
> MUCH PUBLICITY. YOUR SUMMER CAMP IS IN SERI-
> OUS JEOPARDY. I'LL CONTACT AFTER YOU RETURN
> TO THE USA.

June 1963, Newton Center, Massachusetts

A phone call from Mary Pinchot came a week after I returned from Mexico. She was at the Boston airport. She could spend only the afternoon. We met at a seafood restaurant downtown.

"Oh, you reckless Irishman. You got yourself in trouble again. It's magnificent, these headlong calvary charges of yours. *Mais ce n'est pas la guerre.*"

"What'd I do wrong?"

"Publicity. I told you they'd let you do anything you want as long as you kept quiet. The International Federation of Internal Freedom plan was ingenious from all sides. They would have infiltrated every chapter to get some of their people trained. But they're not going to let CBS film you drugging people on the lovely Mexican beach. You could destroy both capitalism and socialism in one month with that sort of thing."

I was struck again by the brittleness this aristocratic woman had picked up from those stern-eyed business-suited WASPS who shuttle from homes to offices in limousines—the information brokers, editors, board members, executive bank officials—youngish men with oldish eyes (faces I used to see around Harvard Square or in the Yale quad) initiated early into the Calvinist conspiracy; sworn to be forever reliable—working for Wild Bill Donovan in Zurich, for Allen Dulles in Washington, for *Life* magnate Henry Luce as bureau chiefs and then shuffling from *Newsweek* to the *Post*—manipulators of secret documents, facts, rumors, estimates, arms inventories, stock margins, voting blocks, industrial secrets; gossip about the sexual and drug preferences of every member of Congress; trained to grab and maintain what they can; all loyal to the Protestant belief that the planet earth sucks.

"Never mind all that," said Mary. "While you've been goofing around, I've been working hard. My friends and I have been turning on some of the most important people in Washington. It's about time we had our own psychedelic cell on the Potomac, don't you think?"

"So you need more drugs? That's going to be a problem. My plans for chemical plants in Mexico got wiped out."

Mary laughed. "Oh, that's no problem. I can give you a contact in England. They'll sell you everything you need. And if things go the way I hope," she said emphatically, "we'll be seeing lots of good drugs produced here at home."

I pressed her, but she declined to say more.

Fall 1963

There came a phone call late one afternoon from Mary Pinchot, her voice tightroping the wire of hysteria. She had rented a car at La Guardia and was now somewhere in Millbrook. She didn't want to come to the estate. Could I meet her in the village?

Driving out the gate, I saw a green Ford parked down Route 44. It followed me. I slowed down. It pulled up behind me. Mary. She climbed in beside me, motioning me to drive on.

I turned down a side road through an unforgettable autumn scene—

golden fields, herds of jet-black cows, trees turning Technicolor, sky glaring indigo—with the bluest girl in the world next to me.

"It was all going so well," she said. "We had eight intelligent women turning on the most powerful men in Washington. And then we got found out. I was such a fool. I made a mistake in recruitment. A wife snitched on us. I'm scared." She burst into tears.

I reached over and stroked her hair. "Is this a result of... I mean, did you have a bad drug experience?"

"No. That's all been perfect. That's why it's so sad. I may be in real trouble. I really shouldn't be here."

"Are you on drugs right now?"

"It's *not me*, it's the situation that's fucked up. You must be very careful now, Timothy. Don't make any waves. No publicity. I'm afraid for you. I'm afraid for all of us."

"Mary," I said soothingly, "Let's go back to the Big House and relax and have some wine and maybe a hot bath and figure out what you should do."

"I know what you're thinking. This is not paranoia. I've gotten mixed up in some dangerous matters. It's real. You've got to believe me." She glared at me. "Do you?"

"Yes I do." Her alarm was convincing me.

"Look, if I ever showed up here suddenly, could you hide me out for awhile?"

"Sure."

"Good." She handed me a pill bottle from her purse. "This is supposed to be the best LSD in the world. From the National Institute of Mental Health. Isn't it funny that I end up giving it to you?"

As I watched her drive away, I wondered. She wasn't breaking any laws. What trouble could she be in?

Winter 1963

Ever since the Kennedy assassination, I had been expecting a phone call from Mary. It came around December 1.

I could hardly understand her. She was either drunk or drugged or overwhelmed with grief. Or all three. "They couldn't control him any more. He was changing too fast."

Long pause. Hysterical crying. I spoke reassurance. She sobbed. "They've covered everything up. I gotta come see you. I'm afraid. Be careful."

The line went dead. Worried, I could do nothing.

1965

I found myself thinking a lot about Mary Pinchot. I asked everyone at Millbrook if she had phoned during my 'round-the-world trip, but no one remembered hearing from her.

Directory assistance in Washington DC had numbers for several Pinchots but none for Mary. Then I remembered that she was a Vassar graduate and phoned the alumni office in Poughkeepsie. The cheery voice of the secretary became guarded when I asked for the address of Mary Pinchot.

"Mary Pinchot?" A long pause. "The person about whom you were asking… ah, her married name is Meyer. But I'm sorry to say that she is… ah… deceased. Sometime last fall, I believe."

"I've been out of the country. I didn't know."

"Thank you for calling," said the alumni secretary.

In shock, I climbed out a third-floor window and up the steep copper roof of the Big House. There I leaned back against a chimney and tried to think things over. Michael Hollingshead, who sensed my malaise, scrambled up to join me, carrying two beers. When I told him about Mary, he brushed away a tear.

"I wonder what happened," I said.

"Next time we go to New York, let's see what we can find out," said Michael. Balancing gracefully on bare feet he walked to the west ledge of the roof to contemplate the setting sun. A flock of swallows swept across the lawn and collected in the branches of the twin birches. I joined him.

So off we went, Michael and I, down the Hudson to New York to meet the light-artists and sound wizards who were popping up on the Lower East Side. And to find out what happened to Mary Pinchot Meyer.

I cabbed over to Van Wolfe's apartment, drank a beer, and asked him if he could get any material on Mary Pinchot Meyer. He made a phone call to a friend who worked for the *New York Times*. An hour later, a messenger was at the door with a manila envelope full of clippings, and WHAM— there was Mary's picture, the pert chin and nose, the deep intense eyes. Above, the headline read: "Woman Painter Shot and Killed on Canal Towpath in Capital. Mrs. Mary Pinchot Meyer was a friend of Mrs. Kennedy. Suspect is arraigned."

Mary had been shot twice in the left temple and once in the chest at 12:45 in the afternoon of October 13, 1964 as she walked along the old Chesapeake and Ohio Canal towpath in Georgetown. A friend told reporters that Mary sometimes walked there with her close friend Jacqueline Kennedy.

Mary's brother-in-law, Benjamin C. Bradlee, *Newsweek's* Washington

Bureau Chief, identified her body. Ben Bradlee was described as having been an intimate of the late President Kennedy. The article also mentioned Mary's ex-husband, Cord Meyer, Jr. Former leader of the American Veterans Committee and the World Federalists, now a government employee, position and agency not specified.

Police said that the motive was apparently robbery or assault. Her purse was found by Ben Bradlee in her home. The suspect, a black male, was being held without bail. He denied the crime. He had been at the canal fishing.

I felt that same vague fear that came when we heard about JFK's assassination.

I was sobbing. I walked to the bathroom and threw cold water on my face. My hands were shaking. I was stunned to learn that Mary had been married to Cord Meyer, my nemesis from graduate school days, who now turned out to be a top spook. My head was spinning with ominous thoughts. A close friend of the Kennedy family had been murdered in broad daylight with no apparent motive. And there had been so little publicity. No outcry. No call for further investigation. I felt that same vague fear that came when we heard about JFK's assassination.

"Can you get me more information?" I asked Van.

Van said he'd contact some of his friends in the police and organized crime to get more facts.

Van came up to Millbrook the next weekend. I took him on a walk to Lunacy Hill. We sat smoking grass, watching the Hudson Valley tint purple as the sun set.

"My friend in police intelligence knew all about the Mary Pinchot Meyer case. Apparently a lot of people are convinced it was an assassination. Two slugs in the brain and one in the body. That's no MO of a rapist. And a mugger isn't going to shoot a woman with no purse in her hand.

Van pulled out a Lucky Strike and lit it. His tremor was more pronounced than usual. "It's gotta be one of the biggest cover-ups in Washington history. It's too hot to handle. Everyone comes out looking bad. Some people say dope was involved. So the truth could hurt everyone, all those powerful people. No one wants the facts known.

"They can't get away with a cover-up like this," I protested.

"They have. And you know what we're going to do? We're going to have the adventure thriller of our lives. We're going to uncover the facts, and you're going to write a book about it. I'll raise some money for Hollingshead to research it in Washington—interview everyone, poke around, bribe maids and precinct cops. Hire private detectives. There are lots of people who might talk."

"I'd just like to know what happened."

Van leaned forward, his whole body shaking. "We'll dig up the facts. But we'll have to get a big publisher behind us to expose a cover-up like this one."

Later that day, I was alone in the dressing room after the performance, missing Nannette or someone, drinking champagne, enjoying the slow let-down of show biz energy, when Michael came in with a worried look. "Van just called. He's upset about something. Wants you to come over."

I found Van chain-smoking Lucky Strikes, emitting panic signals. He had spent the afternoon talking about Mary Pinchot Meyer with a friend, a criminal lawyer. "Manny knew about the case," said Van. "When he heard what we were planning, he hit the roof. He said that acid must have rotted my brain or else I would understand that *nobody* wanted this incident investigated."

"We're not accusing anybody," I said. "And the cover-up is undeniable. All we want is a thorough investigation."

"There are a lot of people who obviously don't."

"So what should we do?"

"Let's lay low. I'll try to raise some money, on the quiet, to pay for the investigation."

It was discouraging.

"Don't be upset," said Van. "The truth comes out sooner or later."

1976

One evening in February, a headline in the San Francisco *Chronicle* caught my eye. "NEW JFK STORY—SEX, POT WITH ARTIST." James Truitt, the source for the sensational story, was identified as a former assistant to Philip Graham, publisher of the Washington *Post*. In interviews with the *National Enquirer,* Associated Press, and Washington *Post* Truitt revealed that a woman named Mary Pinchot Meyer had conducted a two-year love affair with President John Kennedy and had smoked marijuana with him in the White House bedroom. A confidante of Mary Meyer, Truitt told the *Post* correspondent that she and Kennedy met about thirty times between January 1962 and November 1963, when Kennedy was assassinated. Mary Meyer told Truitt that JFK had remarked: "This isn't like cocaine. I'll get you some of that."

Truitt claimed that Mary Meyer kept a diary of her affair with the President, which was found after her death by her sister Toni Bradlee and turned over to James Jesus Angleton, who took the diary to CIA head-quarters and destroyed it. According to the *Post,* "Another source" confirmed that Mary Meyer's diary was destroyed: "This source said the diary… contained a few hundred words of vague reference to an unnamed friend."

Kenneth P. O'Donnell, former White House Appointments Secretary, confirmed that Mary Meyer made visits to the White House but denied allegations of a love affair.

I sensed that Mary Pinchot Meyer's life and death were an important part of modern history. More than we are ever likely to know.

Toni Bradlee was quoted by the Associated Press as saying, "I knew nothing about it when Mary was alive."

According to the *Post,* "Angleton, who resigned as chief of CIA counterintelligence in 1975 following disclosure of some illegal activities by his department, said that Meyer had been a 'cherished friend' of he and his wife. He said that he had assisted the family after Meyer's death in a 'purely private capacity,' also making the funeral arrangements. He refused to say whether there had been a diary."

I lit a Camel, walked to the window, and looked through the jailhouse bars onto San Diego Bay. So it *was* JFK that Mary had been turning on with. Once again I sensed that Mary Pinchot Meyer's life and death were an important part of modern history. More than we are ever likely to know.

EXILE ON BRAIN STREET—A FUTANT'S WELL-LEARNED NEUROPOLITESSE

1972 (written 1977)

A waiter approaches with a steaming silver pot. Leri pours coffee and thick cream in his cup, lights a cigarette and studies the uneasy rippling of fear in his body, the familiar outlaw feeling of helpless pawn on chess board of players with unknown motivations, a commodity bartered by two strange men whom he can see sitting in the lobby talking vigorously. Michel Huachard, the gentlemanly Swiss con artist, is scanning a sheaf of papers.

It is *Monsieur* Hyatt, our discrete government contact, triple agent, and advisor who leads the return, strolling delicately across the dining room followed by Michel whose face is expressionless.

Seated at the table, Hyatt comes to the point directly: "Dear Sir, as a favor to Michel, up until this point I have provided you with information you needed. Now I propose a second round of exchange. I wish to ask you some questions. I have no way of knowing how valuable your answers, if you choose to give them, will be to me. Or how helpful or dangerous they may be to you. Are you willing?"

"Michel is my mentor in this affair," says the Dangerous Fugitive, turning to the Frenchman. "What shall I do?"

Michel Hauchard dabs a handkerchief at the moisture on his forehead. He looks like a fat boy caught in some culinary crime. He seems to have been intimidated by his private conversation with Hyatt.

"I suggest that you cooperate with Monsieur Hyatt."

"Very well," says Leri. "What do you want to know? I trust you are not going to ask silly questions like how many Black Panthers there are in Algeria. Or whether the Weathermen are planning to steal plutonium."

"No," replies Hyatt without smiling. "I want to find out what you think about the danger of drugs."

Body drugs turn on somatic circuits which are ready to be activated. Brain drugs turn on neural circuits that are ready to be activated.

Commodore Leri looks up in surprise and raises his eyebrows.

"Please do not misunderstand," continues Hyatt. "I am not interested in moralizing. I am aware that alcohol, aspirin, hydrocarbons in the atmosphere, and radiation from watching television are far more dangerous physically than any neuro-active drug. And I'm aware that a hundred times more young people are permanently crippled by high school athletics than heroin. Not to mention skiing, mountain climbing, or the bloodbath caused by the promiscuous use of the motorcar by adolescents. No, I want to talk about the psycho-political dangers of drugs."

"Have you read my books?"

Hyatt moves his lips into a tight smile. "I have perhaps not read everything you have written, but I have been able to peruse some detailed summaries which have been prepared by various interested parties. I recall your statement that Lenin could have converted the aristocratic youth of Russia to the revolution without firing a shot, if he had known how to use hashish as a political tool."

"A debatable speculation," smiles the Psychedelic Mutant, "but it may have made the point."

"And what *is* the point?" Hyatt's question comes like a karate chop.

"The point is that brain-reward drugs, in the hands of those who know how to use them, can be a most powerful tool for social change."

"Precisely," says Hyatt sharply. "And there is the danger. As you say, these drugs loosen the connections of the user to society and stimulate internal pleasures within the body and the nervous system. Pleasures that are independent of external rewards and punishments. Isn't it true that brain-reward drugs are basically anti-social and anarchic?"

"My dear Hyatt, are you serious? Certainly you know that everything in nature is anti-social."

"All the more reason for imposing our order on nature," responds Hyatt impassively, testing.

"Our order? Whose order?" asked Leri.

"Our order," repeated Hyatt nervously.

Leri informs: "Body drugs turn on somatic circuits which are ready to be activated. Brain drugs turn on neural circuits that are ready to be activated. The brain, I am sorry to say, is neither social nor anti-social. Transient political regimes create the anti-social. It's the lawmakers and morality police who, from time-to-time and place-to-place, define one experience acceptable and another immoral."

"As it should be," said Hyatt. "You do grant society the right to define the limits of the reality it finds acceptable?"

"The problem is not quite that simple. Just as a regime can restrict what individuals experience, so can individual experiences change regimes."

Hyatt laughs in delight. "You are saying that a society is defined by the drugs it uses? That's a new theory of politics."

"Let's call it neuropolitics. The theory is simple. Drugs can expand and accelerate the use of the brain just as machines expand the scope and power of the muscles. Humanity has used and abused machines. Humanity will use and abuse the expanded possibilities of the brain. Machines and drugs are here to stay. I didn't invent the brain and I didn't invent the botanicals that it feeds on. Sooner or later humanity will learn how to use machines and brain-enhancing drugs."

"Use them for what?"

"That, *Monsieur* Hyatt, is the question. Right, Michel?"

Michel's foxy mind computes the trajectory of the conversation. He begins to laugh. "Here we go again. The prisoner's question."

"What are you two talking about? Have you been nipping these drugs yourself, Michel? What is the question?"

"For the moment," replies Leri, "for your purposes, the question seems to be, what is the purpose of society? The answer to that question determines how you will use machines and drugs."

Hyatt places his elbow on the table, rests his face on his hand and frowns. He shakes his head. "Professor, you have me puzzled. I don't know what to do with you. I feel that you're playing with me frivolously, in that particularly offensive attitude of grinning drugged superiority. And yet what you say intrigues me."

"What about the Sandoz Labs?" says the Scandalous Ex-Professor, grinning.

Religious and philosophic factors are much more important in politics than text books reveal.

"Sandoz!" laughs Hyatt. "Psychochemie AG? The drug company for brain-tickets? LSD by the ton, eh?"

Michel looks blank.

"Sandoz is the Basel lab that discovered LSD," explains Leri.

"You should spend some time with the indole crowd," says Hyatt. "Phone Albert Hofmann. He's eager to meet you. But the indole crew is very elitist. They see themselves as the climax of a long chain of European dialectic mysticism. Generations of gentlemen scholars getting stoned in Berlin villas; generations of blighted grain; ergotism; witches on broomsticks; community orgies; cantons up there in the folds of the Alps that haven't known an unhallucinated day in the last 500 years; keepers of the Gnostic traditions. Christ and Paracelsus were part of the gang. Neurological aristocrats. They don't make waves. They don't tell the youth to turn on and drop out. You do. So what shall we do about you?"

"The kind of question determines the answer. Ask practical questions and you'll get practical answers. As I recall, we got into social philosophy and you started defending society's right to make my brain illegal. What do you want to know?"

"If the policymakers of certain European countries ask me what you think they should do to avoid a drug-abuse problem, what is your answer?"

"They should do exactly the opposite of what the American government did. Let the free market and the laws of supply and demand operate."

"Looking at the results, that sounds sensible. How did the Americans create such a mess?"

"It didn't have to happen. In the early '60s, it became obvious that the next stage of technological evolution, the Information Age, was going to involve neuro-pharmacologicals. Brain drugs were going to play a powerful role in human affairs. The American government was informed of the development and encouraged to sponsor research, factual education and rational control. The President at the time was Jack Kennedy."

"I see what you mean," replies Hyatt.

"The Kennedy family made its fortune distributing Brain Drugs," interjects Michel. "If you call alcohol a Brain Drug?"

"I betray no secret when I say that the Kennedy family was well aware of the positive uses of body-mind drugs and sympathetic to the concept of brain reward."

"He's right," says Michel. "Ask anyone around Gstaad or St. Moritz."

"I know," nods Hyatt. "The role of Dr. Max Jacobson has been a source of considerable amusement among European Intelligence Agencies."

"Who is this Jacobson?" asks Michel. "He sounds Jewish."

"According to my sources," replies Hyatt. "Max Jacobson was a 'speed doctor' who cheerfully energized many show business personalities and later became a member of the Presidential family entourage. Dr. Jake appears in many 'at-home' photos of the Kennedy family. I myself, Michel, have seen pictures of Doctor Jake cheerfully dispensing energy medicine at rest-pauses during President Kennedy's famous fifty-mile 'hike for vigor.'"

"That's my point," says the Exile. "During the Kennedy administration, drug policy was controlled by the Food and Drug Administration, with emphasis placed on research, standards of purity, and the dissemination of rational, scientific information. It's hard to define these issues in political terms, but the Kennedy administration emitted friendly, tolerant vibrations. Openness. Young people, in particular, liked this."

"Yes," muses Hyatt. 'The problem was to appear friendly and be tough at the same time."

Leri replies: "The elevation of Lyndon B. Johnson to the presidency changed many things including the drug policy. Why? Change in presidential religion."

"Religion?" exclaims Michel. "I didn't know Johnson was religious."

"Religious and philosophic factors are much more important in politics than text books reveal. To understand the politics of the 1960s you must remember that LBJ belonged to the Church of Christ."

"You mean he was a puritan Christian?"

"Several historians have suggested that Evangelical Protestantism is the basis for the anti-humanistic mentality which still characterizes the American empire's Holy War fixation."

"Calvinists," cries Michel. "*Pouf!* I detest them."

"The ominous moral defect of Evangelical prudery is that it makes people cruel, vindictive, and unforgiving," muses the Fugitive. "What you wise and tolerant Europeans may not realize is that the American Protestant Fundamentalists are the most unbending, savage and dogmatic, racist, murderous gangs to emerge from the 19th century."

"Red-necked Jansenists?" inquires Hyatt.

"As the more flexible tolerance of the Catholic Kennedy was replaced by Texas fundamentalism, the drug policy shifted from research and medical supervision to highly moralistic control by a new *Kultur-polizei* known as Narcs. In retrospect we can see that the rise to power of men such as Nixon, Haldeman, and Ehrlichman solidified the Puritanical tilt in the American cultural conflict."

"Do you find this interesting, *Monsieur* Hyatt?" asks Michel.

Hyatt smiles. "Do you see this ring? Do you know where it comes from?" Hyatt is holding his pudgy hand in the center of the table to exhibit an ornate gold ring with an enormous ruby surrounded by an Episcopal crown. Michel's watery eyes bulge in astonishment.

"The last and only time I saw a ring like that was at my confirmation. But you, Hyatt?"

The worst mistake a governing regime can make is to place itself in rigid opposition to consumer appetites.

"Let us simply assume that I have done many favors for Rome. Certain congregations in the Vatican are most worried about the manifestations of our Reformed Brethren."

Commodore Leri smiles at the religious wheeler-dealer. 'In the long run, *Monsieur* Hyatt, the worst mistake a governing regime can make is to place itself in rigid opposition to consumer appetites. Governments that attempt to violate the laws of supply and demand are doomed. Laws that attempt to regulate what and whom people put in their own bodies create anti-social and rebellious reactions."

"I repeat. These drugs are by definition anti-social," protests Hyatt.

"If drugs reward and the society punishes, then anti-social feelings are automatically imprinted," replies Leri. "However, if society allows the use of brain-reward drugs then the most enthusiastic patriotic reactions will result."

"You're talking about Brave New World."

"I'm talking about the bio-neurology of the human being, *Monsieur* Hyatt. In the last analysis, the basic satisfactions that humanity buys with the money earned by work are biological and neurological. Food. Shelter. Health. Pleasure. Bliss. A fundamental need of humanity is the neurological experience we call intoxication, the cyclical hunger to alter consciousness, to bend reality, to stimulate the brain bored with routine. Certainly our most rigidly organized social institution, the military, understands this need. Alcohol is unashamedly used as the official off-duty reward. And look at the Japanese who can always be counted on to provide us with caricature exaggerations of the trends of technological culture. Japanese executives are permitted, encouraged, even required to get staggeringly, flamboyantly drunk in *ginza* bars after work."

Hyatt drums his fingers on the linen tablecloth and shakes his head at Michel Hauchard.

"Just as I feared. Our hero with the New Elixir of Life is indeed dangerous and is therefore in danger. You see, like it or not, the dehumanization which you say stems from evangelic Protestantism has effectively conquered the world. Let's face facts. There are few countries that are not rushing headlong into assembly-line homogeneity. Too bad for you, Doctor. A few decades ago—when sultans, kings, warlords, aristocrats, philosophers, and colonial governors ran the world, you would have found several eccentric potentates that would be fascinated to sponsor your ingenuous theories and who would give you shelter. But today the industrial world has been organized by the Cold War into monolithic blocks. The psychology of nations is now determined by their Cold War status. You are absolutely antagonistic and dangerous to any and all governments. Look what drugs did in Vietnam! A half-million American troops rendered serenely non-belligerent because of the high-grade marijuana and heroin. History may well decide that the American empire was defeated at the high-water mark of its expansion by a decline of martial ardor produced by dope. I can assure you, *Monsieur Leri*, that no government in the world will allow you refuge."

* * * * *

Timothy Francis Leary 1920–1996

West Point, 1940.

1920

Born October 22, 1920, Springfield, MA.

1929

Leary's father, Tote, runs away from home.

1940s

West Point cadet. Subjected to "silencing" punishment for drinking with upper classmen and then lying about it before administrators.

Expelled from University of Alabama for sleeping in girl's dormitory.

Marries first wife, Marianne.

Earns doctorate at UC Berkeley in Psychology.

Director of Psychology Research at Kaiser Foundation in Berkeley.

Birth of daughter Susan and son Jack.

1950s

Leads notorious swinger lifestyle in Berkeley with wife, Marianne.

Marianne commits suicide on Leary's 35th birthday.

Publication of *The Interpersonal Diagnosis of Personality*. Book is well-received and influential. Advocates equal relationship between psychiatrist and client.

Hired in 1959 as lecturer in Psychology at Harvard to bring fresh ideas and stir things up.

1960

Takes psilocybin in Mexico and has revelatory experience.

Returns to Harvard and starts Harvard Psilocybin Research Project. Joined by fellow Professor Richard Alpert (later "Baba Ram Dass").

Lecturing on "The Interpersonal Diagnosis of Personality" in the late 1950s.

Leary shares psilocybin with Allen Ginsberg. They agree to change the world with psychedelic drugs.

1960–1963

With the Harvard Psilocybin Research Project, Leary conducts research with well-known creative artists, priests, prisoners, and students, with mostly positive therapeutic results.

1961

Professor Leary tries the more powerful psychedelic LSD. The experience awes him.

Leary and Ginsberg turn on artists to psilocybin, including William S. Burroughs, Robert Lowell, and Charles Mingus.

Mid '60s, probably at Millbrook.

1962

As public controversy spreads about the Psilocybin Research Project's work at Harvard; Leary and Alpert form the International Foundation for Internal Freedom (IFIF) to promote the idea that the right to psychedelic experiences is a basic civil liberty.

With Allen Ginsberg, Peggy Hitchcock, Lawrence Ferlinghetti (early 1960s).

1963

Richard Alpert fired by Harvard for sharing drugs with students. Leary gets himself fired by not showing up for classes.

Psychedelic experiments continue at mansion in Millbrook, New York provided by wealthy heirs, Billy and Tommy Hitchcock.

1964

Ken Kesey and his Merry Pranksters ride a psychedelic bus across America dressed in superhero costumes. They visit Millbrook but find it too sedate.

Leary marries model Nena von Schlebrugge in a big psychedelic ceremony at Millbrook. The marriage is filmed by D.A.

With Rosemary Woodruff Leary, circa 1967.

Pennebaker and photographed by Dianne Arbus. (von Schlebrugge would later marry Robert Thurman, a leading expert in Tibetan Buddhism, and give birth to actress Uma Thurman.)

Leary, Alpert and Ralph Metzner write *Psychedelic Experience*, a re-interpretation of the *Tibetan Book of the Dead*

1965

Leary and von Schlebrugge divorce.

Leary meets and falls in love with future wife Rosemary Woodruff.

In an apparent set-up, Leary, Rosemary Woodruff and daughter Susan arrested for possession of a few grams of marijuana in Laredo, Texas at Mexican border. Leary takes responsibility for the pot. Bail is set at $100,000.

Leary sentenced to thirty years in prison based on Laredo bust. Eighteen-year-old daughter Susan Leary sentenced to five years. Both are released on bail pending appeal.

1966

A drug raid at Millbrook is led by Dutchess County, New York Prosecutor G. Gordon Liddy. Leary is taken to jail, but the suspect substance turns out to be peat moss.

Leary announces slogan: "Turn On, Tune In, Drop Out."

Leary testifies before a Senate investigation into the dangers of LSD.

The Death of the Mind, a theatrical performance written by and starring Leary runs for six weeks in the East Village, receiving positive reviews and solid attendance. Attempts at follow-up theatrical pieces will be poorly received.

1967

Leary joins Alan Watts, Gary Snyder, Allen Ginsberg, the Grateful Dead and others on the stage for the First Human Be-In in Golden Gate Park in San Francisco.

Leary marries Rosemary Woodruff in a ceremony filmed by Ted Markus, the director of the popular TV show Bonanza.

Mid 1960s. Another attempted G. Gordon Liddy raid on Millbrook while Leary, friends and family are away finds no drugs.

1968

Millbrook scene closes down. Leary and family move to Berkeley, California.

Moody Blues release song about Timothy Leary, "Legend of a Mind."

Leary supports—and then withdraws support from—planned antiwar demonstrations at Chicago Democratic Convention with the Yippies—a New Left-meets-psychedelia activist organization headed by Abbie Hoffman, Jerry Rubin, and Paul Krassner.

Leary's two most popular books, High Priest and The Politics of Ecstasy are released.

Leary and entire family are busted while smoking pot in a car while visiting Laguna Beach, California. This time, police also find hashish, LSD and Ritalin.

1969

Leary wins Laredo case before US Supreme Court challenging the "marijuana tax" as unconstitutional on the grounds that it requires self-incrimination. At the press conference, he announces he's running for Governor of California against Ronald Reagan.

Timothy and Rosemary Leary join John Lennon and Yoko Ono for their "Bed-In For

Peace" in Montreal.

John Lennon writes "Come Together" for Leary gubernatorial campaign.

Prosecutors re-file charges against Leary for the Laredo bust based on a technicality. They are now seeking a twenty-year sentence.

1970

Leary sentenced to ten years in prison and a $10,000 fine for the Laguna Beach bust. He is remanded to prison without bail. The sentencing judge denounces him as "an irresponsible Madison Avenue advocate of the free use of LSD and marijuana."

Leary escapes from a California prison with the assistance of the Weather Underground and Brotherhood of Eternal Love.

Entering prison in 1970.

Leary and wife Rosemary join Black Panther Party exile chapter in Algeria, under the leadership of Eldridge Cleaver.

Eldridge Cleaver puts the Learys under "house arrest" for not following orders. They escape Algeria with help from the Algerian government.

In exile in Switzerland, 1971.

1971–72

The Learys live in Switzerland under temporary protection. They are provided for—and ripped off by—shady Eurotrash criminal Michel Huachard.

1972

Leary held briefly in prison in Switzerland while Swiss government contemplates U.S. request for extradition. He is released.

Rosemary Leary leaves.

Leary begins affair with French-Hungarian jet-set heiress Joanna Harcourt-Smith.

Leary named as "key figure" in bust of drug dealers The Brotherhood of Eternal Love for sales of massive amounts of LSD, hashish, and hash oil. Bail *in absentia* is set at $5,000,000, the hightest in U.S. history up to that point.

1973

In what may have been a set-up by insiders, Leary is illegally captured by United States Federal Bureau of Narcotics and Dangerous Drugs while visiting Afghanistan with Joanna and other friends. He is returned to Folsom Prison. Charles Manson is in the cell next door. At 53, he now faces 95 years in prison.

Publication of *Confessions of a Hope Fiend,* story of prison, prison escape (minus details), and exile with Black Panthers.

Publication of *Starseed*—monograph about potential for space travel and extraterrestrial contact.

Publication of *Neurologic*—completion of Leary's theory of brain circuitry and human evolution.

Leary is admitted to Vacaville, an acute-care psychiatric hospital for the criminally insane.

Leary agrees to tell the FBI the details of his escape from prison.

1974

Leftist radicals, including Jerry Rubin, denounce Leary in Berkeley, California press conference.

A planned armed escape—with help from Joanna—while being driven around by FBI agents on a supposed search for Weather Underground "safe houses" ends when Leary realized he can't shoot anybody.

Circa 1976: Leary, Joanna Harcourt-Smith (right), unknown woman in b.g.

1975

The statute of limitations runs out and the FBI fails to get indictments based on Leary's testimony.

Leary is thrown into solitary in Minnesota prison when he refuses to be released among the general population under the name "Charles Thrush."

Top L to R: Oscar Janiger, Laura Huxley, John Lilly
Bottom L to R: Nina Graboi, Leary, Carolyn Kleefeld

Janiger, Huxley, and Lilly were all associated with serious psychedelic research; Graboi was long involved in Leary's various organizations.

1976

Under pressure from the Jerry Brown administration, the California Prison Authority releases Leary on probation. He refuses to be part of the "Witness Protection Program."

Emerges as early Transhumanist, advocating Space Migration, Intelligence Increase, and Life Extension. (SMI2LE)

Publication of *What Does WoMan Want?*, fictionalized biography mostly focused on exile in Switzerland. It is the first of five books—mostly written in prison—known as the "Future History Series,"

1977

Leary moves to Los Angeles. Tours as "Stand-Up Philospher."

Publication of *Neuropolitics: The Sociobiology of Human Metamorphosis,* a collection of essays and part of "Future History Series."

Publication of *Exo-Psychology, a Manual on the Use of the Human Nervous System According to the instructions of the Manufacturers.* Part of "Future History Series."

1978

Leary marries Barbara Chase, occasional filmmaker and full-time scenemaker.

Publishes *The Intelligence Agents.* ("Future History Series.")

With Burroughs in Lawrence, Kansas, circa early '90s.

1979

Leary lectures at a Libertarian Party conference about the coming of the Internet and personal autonomy.

Publication of *The Game of Life*. The book maps correspondences between Leary's system of Neurologic, Crowleyan magick, and the Periodic Table of Elements, among other things. It is the last of the "Future History Series."

1980s

Leary becomes part of evolving computer culture. He is particularly an advocate for William Gibson's *Neuromancer*. He advocates a cyberpunk movement—Do It Yourself with technology. The new slogan is "Turn On. Tune In. Take Over."

Leary tours with former nemesis, G. Gordon Liddy, for big bucks.

Publication of *Changing My Mind, Among Others,* a collection of writings in 1982.

Publication of *Flashbacks,* an autobiography, in 1983. The book receives favorable reviews and somewhat revives Leary's reputation

Release of "Mind Mirror," computer role-playing game in 1985.

In 1989, Leary becomes contributing editor of new technoculture magazine, *Mondo 2000*.

In 1989, Leary's daughter Susan commits suicide, hanging herself in prison, where she is being held for shooting her boyfriend.

1990s

Leary's wife Barbara leaves him.

New slogan for the '90s:"Think For Yourself and Question Authority."

Leary is informed that he is dying of prostate cancer. He turns his dying process into a massive publicity campaign against taboos around death. He announces that he will die on the Internet and that his head will be severed and cryogenically preserved.

Publication of *Chaos and Cyberculture,* a collection of writings from the '80s and '90s.

1996

Leary dies quietly among friends and family, May 31, in Los Angeles. His ashes are sent into space along with the ashes of Gene Roddenberry and Gerard K. O'Neill (spokesman for an influential theory of how to colonize space).

Circa early 1990s.

Circa 1995.

RE/SEARCH CATALOG

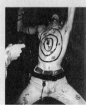

PUNK & D.I.Y.

PUNK '77: an inside look at the San Francisco rock n' roll scene, 1977 by James Stark

Covers the beginnings of the S.F. Punk Rock scene through the Sex Pistols' concert at Winterland in Jan., 1978, in interviews and photographs by James Stark. James was among the many artists involved in early punk. His photos were published in *New York Rocker, Search & Destroy* and *Slash,* among others. His posters for Crime are classics. Over 100 photos, including many behind-the-scenes looks at the bands who made things happen: Nuns, Avengers, Crime, Screamers, Negative Trend, Dils, Germs, UXA, etc. Interviews with the bands and people early on the scene give intimate, often darkly humorous glimpses of events in a *Please Kill Me* (Legs McNeil) style. "The photos themselves, a generous 115 of them, are richly satisfying. They're the kind of photos one wants to see..."—*Puncture.* "I would recommend this book not only for old-timers looking for nostalgia, but especially to young Punks who have no idea how this all got off the ground, who take today's Punk for granted, to see how precarious it was at birth, what a fluke it was, and to perhaps be able to get a fresh perspective on today's scene."—*MAXIMUMROCKNROLL* 7½x10¼", 98 pp, 100+ photos, on archival art paper. PB, $20

SEARCH & DESTROY: The Complete Reprint (2 big 10x15" volumes)

Vol. 1 out of print

"The best punk publication ever"—Jello Biafra

Facsimile editions (at 90% size) include all the interviews, articles, ads, illustrations and photos. Captures the enduring revolutionary spirit of punk rock, 1977–1978. Published by V. Vale before his RE/Search series, *Search & Destroy* is a definitive, first-hand documentation of the punk rock cultural revolution, printed as it happened! Patti Smith, Iggy Pop, Ramones, Sex Pistols, Clash, DEVO, Avengers, Mutants, Dead Kennedys, William S. Burroughs, J.G. Ballard, John Waters, Russ Meyer, and David Lynch (to name a few) offer permanent inspiration and guidance. First appearance of Bruce Conner Punk photos. 10x15", 148pp. Vol. 1 o.p., Vol. Two: $19.95. **Search & Destroy original tabloid issues are still available. Call or email for information.**

INDUSTRIAL CULTURE HANDBOOK DELUXE HARDBACK

This book is a secret weapon—it provided an educational upbringing for many of the most radical artists practicing today! The rich ideas of the Industrial Culture movement's performance artists and musicians are nakedly exposed: Survival Research Laboratories, Throbbing Gristle, Cabaret Voltaire, SPK, Non, Monte Cazazza, Johanna Went, Sordide Sentimental, R&N, & Z'ev. Topics include: brain research, forbidden medical texts & films, creative crime & interesting criminals, modern warfare & weaponry, neglected gore films & their directors, psychotic lyrics in past pop songs, and art brut. Limited Edition hardbacks on glossy paper. 8½x11", 140 pp, 179 photos & illust. PB, $40.

ZINES Vol. 1 & 2

The Punk Rock Principle of "DO-IT-YOURSELF" (D-I-Y) inspired the creation of "ZINES": handmade self-publications by creative individuals, usually exhibiting personal viewpoints and against status quo thinking and ideas. *Murder Can Be Fun, Beer Frame, Crap Hound, Thrift Score, Bunny Hop, Fat Girl, Housewife Turned Assassin* gleefully show the satisfactions to be had by "publishing it yourself." These two books will inspire and provoke readers to become publishers. Have been used as college textbooks. Heavily illustrated with photographs and illustrations from Zinemakers' lives & works. Zines 1: 184 pp, 8½x11", PB, $18.99. Zines 2: 148 pp, PB, $14.99. **GET BOTH for $20.00 (plus shipping for two items).**

BODY MODIFICATION AND S&M

RE/Search 12: MODERN PRIMITIVES

The New York Times called this "the Bible of the underground tattooing and body piercing movement." Modern Primitives launched an entire '90s subculture. Crammed with illustrations & information, it's now considered a classic. The best texts on ancient human decoration practices such as tattooing, piercing, scarification and more. 279 eye-opening photos and graphics; 22 in-depth interviews with some of the most colorful people on the planet. "Dispassionate ethnography that lets people put their behavior in its own context."—*Voice Literary Supplement* "The photographs and illustrations are both explicit and astounding . . . provides fascinating food for thought. —*Iron Horse* 8½x11", 212 pp, 279 photos and illus, PB. Great gift! $19.50

Confessions of Wanda von Sacher-Masoch

Married for 10 years to Leopold von Sacher-Masoch (author: Venus in Furs & many other novels) whose whip-and-fur bedroom games spawned the term "masochism," Wanda's story is a feminist classic from 100 years ago. She was forced to play "sadistic" roles in Leopold's fantasies to ensure the survival of herself & their 3 children–games which called into question who was the Master and who the Slave. Besides being a compelling story of a woman's search for her own identity, strength and, ultimately, complete independence, this is a true-life adventure story–an odyssey through many lands peopled by amazing characters. Here is a woman's consistent unblinking investigation of the limits of morality and the deepest meanings of love. "Extravagantly designed in an illustrated, oversized edition that is a pleasure to hold. It is also exquisitely written, engaging and literary and turns our preconceptions upside down."—L.A. Reader 8½x11", 136 pp, illustrated, PB. $20

The Torture Garden by Octave Mirbeau

This book was once described as the "most sickening work of art of the nineteenth century!" Long out of print, Octave Mirbeau's macabre classic (1899) features a corrupt Frenchman and an insatiably cruel Englishwoman who meet and then frequent a fantastic 19th century Chinese garden where torture is practiced as an art form. The fascinating, horrific narrative slithers deep into the human spirit, uncovering murderous proclivities and demented desires. "Hot with the fever of ecstatic, prohibited joys, as cruel as a thumbscrew and as luxuriant as an Oriental tapestry. Exotic, perverse . . . hailed by the critics."—Charles Hanson Towne 8½x11", 120 pp, 21 mesmerizing photos.

PB: $25. Rare Hardcover (edition of only 100; treat yourself!): $40

Bob Flanagan Super Masochist

Born 1952 and deceased in 1996, Bob grew up with Cystic Fibrosis, and discovered extended S&M practices as a secret, hand-picked pathway towards life extension. In flabbergastingly detailed interviews, Bob described his sexual practices and his relationship with long-term partner and Mistress, the artist Sheree Rose. Through his insider's perspective we learn about branding, piercing, whipping, bondage and ingenious, improvised endurance trials. Includes photographs by Sheree Rose. This book "inspired" a movie, which used many of the questions found in this book. "...an elegant tour through the psychic terrain of SM." —*Details Magazine* 8½x11", 136 pp, illustrated, PB. $20.00

PRANKS

RE/Search 11: PRANKS!

A prank is a "trick, a mischievous act, a ludicrous act." Although not regarded as poetic or artistic acts, pranks constitute an art form and genre in themselves. Here pranksters challenge the sovereign authority of words, images and behavioral convention. This iconoclastic compendium will dazzle and delight all lovers of humor, satire and iron. "I love this book. I thought I was the only weirdo out there, but this book inspires me to be weirder. I pick it up weekly, even though I've read it from covr to cover many times. Still cracks me up." (reader) "The definitive treatment of the subject, offering extensive interviews with 36 contemporary tricksters including Henry Rollins, Abbie Hoffman, Jello Biafra, SRL, Karen Finley, John Waters, DEVO . . . from the Underground's answer to Studs Terkel."—Washington Post 8½x11″, 240 pp, 164 photos & illustrations, PB, $25, Deluxe HB $40.

PRANKS 2

"Pranks woke me up from a deep slumber. It's as if a demolition crew had a party in my brain." (reader) An extended underground of surrealist artists like The Suicide Club, Billboard Liberation Front, DEVO, John Waters, Lydia Lunch & Monte Cazazza give inspiring tales of mirth and conceptual mayhem. Includes Internet pranks, art pranks, prank groups and more! 81x10″, 200 pp,, many photos & illustrations, PB, glossy paper, 8x10″, $20.

TWO BY DANIEL P. MANNIX

MEMOIRS OF A SWORD SWALLOWER

Not for the faint-of-heart, this book will GROSS SOME PEOPLE OUT and delight others. "I probably never would have become America's leading fire-eater if Flamo the Great hadn't happened to explode that night . . ." So begins this true story of life with a traveling carnival, peopled by amazing characters—the Human Ostrich, the Human Salamander, Jolly Daisy, etc.—who commit outrageous feats of wizardry. One of the only authentic narratives revealing the "tricks" (or rather, painful skills) involved in a sideshow, and is invaluable to those aspiring to this profession. OVER 50 RARE PHOTOS taken by Mannix in the 1930s. 8½x11″, 128 pp, 50+ photos, index, PB, **$20, $30 Signed**

FREAKS: We Who Are Not As Others

Amazing Photos! This book engages the reader in a struggle of wits: Who is the freak? What is normal? What are the limits of the human body? A fascinating, classic book, based on Mannix's personal acquaintance with sideshow stars such as the Alligator Man and the Monkey Woman. Read all about the notorious love affairs of midgets; the amazing story of the Elephant Boy; the unusual amours of Jolly Daisy, the fat woman; hermaphrodite love; the bulb-eating Human Ostrich, etc. **Put this on your coffee table and watch the fun!** 8½x11″, 124 pp, 88 photos. PB. **$20** Author died in 1997. **Signed, hardbound copies available for $50**

J.G. BALLARD

J.G. Ballard: Quotes

Amazing, provocative quotes from J..G. Ballard illuminating the human condition, arranged by topic. Edited by V. Vale with Mike Ryan. Dozens of gorgeous photos by Ana Barrado, Charles Gatewood and others. "Ballard understands the transformation technology can effect on human desire." —*Observer*
ISBN 1-889307-12-2, 416 pages, index, 5" x 7", gloss paper, $20. Limited AUTOGRAPHED Flexibind Edition of only 250 copies, signed by J.G. Ballard himself, only $75. Also, unsigned Library Flexibind Editions (only 100 printed) available, only $35.

J.G. Ballard Conversations

British luminary, J.G. Ballard converses with V. Vale, Mark Pauline, Graeme Revell, David Pringle and other forward thinkers. Photographs by Ana Barrado, Charles Gatewood and others. Some topics: Sex, technology, the future, plastic surgery, child-raising, Empire of the Sun. Index, book recommendations, and interviews are also included.
ISBN 1-889307-13-0, 360 pages, index, 5" x 7", gloss paper, $20

RE/Search 8/9: J.G. Ballard

J.G. Ballard is our finest living visionary writer. His classic, CRASH (made into a movie by David Cronenberg) was the first book to investigate the psychopathological implications of the car crash, uncovering our darkest sexual crevices. He accurately predicted our media-saturated, information-overloaded environment where our most intimate fantasies and dreams involve pop stars and other public figures. Intvs, texts, critical articles, bibliography, biography.

Also contains a wide selection of quotations. "Highly recommended as both an introduction and a tribute to this remarkable writer."—*Washington Post* "The most detailed, probing and comprehensive study of Ballard on the market."—*Boston Phoenix*.
8½x11", 176 pp, illus. PB. $20 (last copies; order soon!)

Atrocity Exhibition

A dangerous imaginary work; as William Burroughs put it, "This book stirs sexual depths untouched by the hardest-core illustrated porn." Amazingly perverse medical illustrations by Phoebe Gloeckner, and haunting "Ruins of the Space Age" photos by Ana Barrado. Our most beautiful book, now used in many "Futurology" college classes. 8½x11", 136 pp, illus. PB $20. LIMITED EDITION OF SIGNED HARDBACKS $150 (Only 20 copies left)

W.S. BURROUGHS

R/S 4/5: WS Burroughs, Brion Gysin, Throbbing Gristle
A great, unknown Burroughs-Gysin treasure trove of radical ideas!
Compilation of interviews, scarce fiction, essays: this is a manual of incendiary insights. Strikingly designed; bulging with radical references.
Topics discussed: biological warfare, utopias, con men, lost inventions, the JFK killing, Hassan I Sabbah, cloning, the cut-up theory, Moroccan trance music, the Dream Machine, Manson, the media control process, prostitution, and more. 8½x11", 100 pp, 58 photos & illus. Lim Ed. Hardback of only 500 copies, Special $40 Order Direct! PB $20.

T-shirt!

William S. Burroughs T-shirt!
with photo by Ruby Ray
Black & red on white "We intend to destroy all dogmatic verbal systems."—WSB.
Original design hand-screened on 100% heavyweight cotton T-Shirt. **$25**

Burroughs Special: #4/5 Deluxe HB, T-shirt, Search & Destroy #10 (with Burroughs interview) PLUS full (front & back) original #4/5 bookcover/poster. $70 plus shipping (for 2 items).

T-SHIRTS

hirt!

RE/Search Logo T-shirts are back! $25
Black and white and "read" all over
On back: "Media Against the Status Quo"
Black shirts, red printing or black shirts, red and white printing
on 100% cotton knit.

Mr Death T-Shirt by Man-Woman.
Black & yellow on White 100% heavyweight cotton T-Shirt. Sizes: S,M,L,XL.
Limited edition, 50 copies: $25.

Mr Death
Tshirt!

T-shirt!

T-shirt!

SPECIAL OFFER: MODERN PRIMITIVES BOOK & T-SHIRT GIFT-PACK—ONLY $29.00 PLUS SHIPPING.

Modern Primitives T-shirt!
Multi-color on black 100% cotton T-shirt
Illustrations of 12 erotic piercings and implants. **$16.**

POLLINATOR PRESS

True Mutations: Interviews on the Edge of Science, Technology, and Consciousness by R. U. Sirius

looks at the wild changes that may be coming to the human species during the 21st century. In a series of interviews, author/host RU Sirius explores (r)evolutions in disciplines ranging from the evolution of clean energy to the possibilities of endless neurological ecstasy; from open-source free access to nearly everything under the sun to self-directed biotechnological evolution; from psychedelic culture mash-ups to the possibilities of a technological singularity that alters not only humanity but the entire universe Includes: Genesis P-Orridge, Cory Doctorow, DJ Spooky, Robert Anton Wilson, Jaron Lanier, Dan Pinchbeck. 6x9", 304 pp, PB, $20.

Five Fingers Make a Fist by Alexander Laurence.

Laurence has taken storytelling as the subject of his book. Five Fingers Make A Fist juxtaposes extreme realism, science, poetry and theater in 28 stories told through various points of view, from a baby narrator in "My Birth" to an old lady waiting to die in "The Ballad of Nariyama." Many of the stories take place in San Francisco in the 1990s, yet they are truly universal. Inspired by pop culture, music, and TV, these stories are too entertaining for any literature to get in the way (it's okay if you don't get the literary references and in-jokes the first time). The characters become so twisted by their own self invention that they start to believe their own made up stories about themselves and the world. Sometimes their self-made fantasy becomes a truer version. What is real? What is a mask? Prepare to have the world turned upside down. PB, $14.95

10 Birds with 1 Stone by Merritt Sher

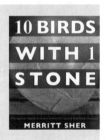

In a handy, pocketsize package, 10 Birds with 1 Stone offers fifty-two carefully honed teachings that can be appreciated quickly, often and over and over again, read straight through or opened randomly to any page. At one level, the book can be studied like a concentrated MBA course for its seasoned advice on how to succeed in business. But its deeper insights sneak up on you like the wisdom of a Sufi Master. This isn't just about business. It's a philosophy of life that downloads to a system for self-realization and fulfillment that's for anyone who wants to create and evolve. $14.95 PB, $19.99 deluxe hardback.

RE/SEARCH PUBLICATIONS
20 ROMOLO #B
SAN FRANCISCO, CA 94133
tel (415) 362-1465
EMAIL: *info@researchpubs.com*
www.researchpubs.com
See more of our content and products online.
Order from our secure server.

RUDOS & RUBES PRESS

The Guilt of the Templars by G. Legman.

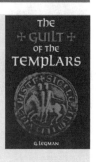

Contributions from Henry Charles Lea, Thomas Wright, George Witt, Sir James Tennent and Sir William Dugdale. One of the rarest works of the late Gershon Legman (1917–1999), bibliographer for the Kinsey Institute and author of Rationale of the Dirty Joke and Love & Death. Drawing on actual depositions and confessions of the Templars and probing deeper than the religious, financial, or political issues, Mr. Legman's searching analysis of the effects of supressing normal sexuality remains a unique and brilliant interpretation of the nature of the Templars' guilt. Many extras, including the 1309 proceedings against the Order, translated by Sir William Dugdale. 260 pages, PB, $15.95.

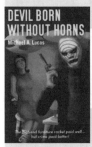

Devil Born Without Horns by Michael Lucas

Darkly humorous, at times brutal tale of crime and conspicuous consumption in the high-end furniture industry. 286 pages, PB, $10.95.

A Loud Humming Sound Came From Above by Johnny Strike

features the genre-bending, hallucinatory style that distinguishes his novel, Ports of Hell. Twelve short stories on the edge of science fiction and J.G. Ballard. Illustrations by Richard Sala. 165 pages, PB, $12.95.

Raw Rumbles by Hal Ellson

These three classic "juvenile-delinquent" (J.D.) novels, had been out-of-print, until this collection published for the next generations. Duke (1949), Tomboy (1950), The Knife (1951). 350 pages, PB, $19.95.

VISIT WWW.RESEARCHPUBS.COM TO SEE MORE OF OUR BOOKS, CDS AND VIDEOS!

JOIN THE RE/SEARCH ENEWSLETTER LIST FOR MONTHLY UPDATES OR FIND US AT WWW. RESEARCHPUBS.COM

Visa/MC, check, money order
or paypal accepted.
info@researchpubs.com

SHIPPING USA: $5 per item, Add $2/item for Priority Mail USA.
Overseas Global Air: $15 per item.
Contact us with questions or requests!

INDEX

M

N

O

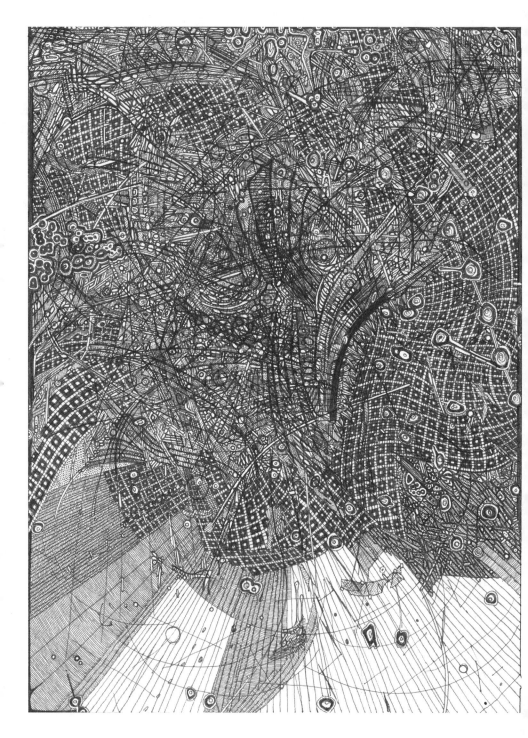